REFUGEE CRISIS IN INTERNATIONAL POLICY

VOLUME III

REFUGEE POLICIES OF THE INTERNATIONAL ORGANIZATIONS

REFUGEE CRISIS IN INTERNATIONAL POLICY

VOLUME III

REFUGEE POLICIES OF THE INTERNATIONAL ORGANIZATIONS

Edited by

Hasret Çomak, Burak Şakir Şeker, Mehlika Özlem Ultan,
Yaprak Civelek, Çağla Arslan Bozkuş

TRANSNATIONAL PRESS LONDON

2021

MIGRATION SERIES: 30

Refugee Crisis in International Policy, Volume III - Refugee Policies of the International Organizations

Edited by Hasret Çomak, Burak Şakir Şeker, Mehlika Özlem Ultan, Yaprak Civelek, Çağla Arslan Bozkuş

First Published in 2021 by TRANSNATIONAL PRESS LONDON in the United Kingdom, 13 Stamford Place, Sale, M33 3BT, UK. www.tplondon.com

Transnational Press London® and the logo and its affiliated brands are registered trademarks.

Requests for permission to reproduce material from this work should be sent to: sales@tplondon.com

Paperback
ISBN: 978-1-80135-014-3
Digital
ISBN: 978-1-80135-015-0

Cover Design: Nihal Yazgan
Cover Photo by Katie Rodriguez, Unsplash.com

Transnational Press London Ltd. is a company registered in England and Wales No. 8771684

CONTENTS

PREFACE

Every day, in many parts of the world people are giving the hardest decisions of their lives. With these decisions, they have to leave their homes behind for a better and safer life. Many people in the world, by giving the decision to leave where they grew up, move to a close settlement. Some have to leave their country for a short period of time or for a lifetime.

In many parts of the world, there are many reasons why people try to re-establish their lives in other countries. Some leave their home country to find a job or for education. Others are forced to escape from human rights violations such as inhuman treatment and torture. Millions run away from armed conflicts or violence. These people who do not feel safe; might be targeted due to their characteristics that establish their identity or faith such as their ethnic origin, religious beliefs, gender, and political thoughts.

These journeys that have begun in pursuit of a better future, might be full of danger and fear; some might fall into the trap of human traffickers or other forms of exploitation. Also, some are taken into custody by authorities as soon as they arrive in a country. Many, who settle in a country and start a new life face racism, xenophobia, and discrimination almost every day. They may feel lonely and isolated.

There are many reasons which make it difficult and dangerous for people to stay in their country of origin. Violence, war, hunger, and poverty are the most important ones. Sexual preferences and sexual identity also take an important place. People may also have to leave their home country because of climate change and natural disasters. Mostly, it is possible to encounter many of these difficult conditions all at once.

Fleeing danger is not the only reason people leave their country. Some think of becoming a part of a qualified workforce or gain capital in another country. Moreover, they suppose there is a higher possibility of finding a job in a foreign country. Others seek to live with their relatives and friends currently living abroad. Also, there might be those who aim to begin and continue their education in another country. Therefore, there are many reasons why people might start out to establish a new life in another country.

It is noteworthy to mention the words "refugee", "asylum seeker" and "migrant" in terms of International Law. The refugee is the person who leaves his home country due to the threat of being subjected to grave human rights violations and persecution. These people have to leave their home country and seek asylum in another country due to security threats and threats against their lives. As they have no other choice and they feel their governments cannot or will not protect them against these threats, they are forced to take this decision.

According to the provisions of the "United Nations Convention Relating to the Status of Refugees", adopted on 28 July 1951 by the United Nations Conference of Plenipotentiaries on the Status of Refugees and Stateless Persons convened under General Assembly resolution 429 (V) of 14 December 1950 and entered into force on 22 April 1954, refugees have "the right for international protection".

An asylum seeker is a person who has left his home country to seek asylum in another country to be protected from persecution and grave human rights violations. However, in this case, one only has the status of asylum applicants and legally has not yet been accepted as a refugee. Seeking an asylum application is a human right. This means everyone should be given permission to enter a country to seek asylum.

Migrants, on the other hand, are those who live outside their home country thus who are not asylum seekers or refugees. Migrants in general, leave their home countries to work, to have an education, or to live with their family members in another country. Some feel the need to leave their home country for the reasons of poverty, political turmoil, natural disasters, or other difficult conditions.

The issue that should be emphasized here is the situation that many people who do not fit into the "refugee" definition might get be in danger once they are returned to their home country. Even if they may not be escaping from persecution, no matter what their legal status is in the country they established themselves, migrants' human rights must be protected, and these rights must be respected.

States must protect all migrants against violence based on racism and xenophobia, exploitation, and forced labor. Migrants should not be detained without legitimate reasons or forcefully send back to their home country.

Human rights have become both a subject and a legitimate instrument of international politics. Therefore, the human rights of refugees, asylum seekers and migrants must always be protected at the international level. States must fulfill their joint responsibility to protect the rights of refugees, asylum seekers and migrants.

People are not the source of the problem. The main problem is the reasons that force families and individuals to cross borders. Those who cause these reasons have responsibilities. The attitude of authorities who are trying far-sighted and unrealistic approaches matters in the creation of this problem.

States must ensure that refugees, asylum seekers and immigrants are safe, not subject to torture, discrimination and living in poverty.

States should assess the applications of asylum seekers according to international rules except for the ones who;

- has committed a crime against peace, a war crime, or a crime against humanity, as defined in the international instruments drawn up to make provision in respect of such crimes;
- has committed a serious non-political crime outside the country of refuge prior to his admission to that country as a refugee;
- has been guilty or suspicious of acts contrary to the purposes and principles of the United Nations.

The situation of asylum seekers should not be left in a state of uncertainty for years. Unlawful detention practices should not be carried out and the necessary diligence should be taken in this regard. Also, international regulations must be made in order to protect migrants against the exploitation of employers or human traffickers and abuse.

States must take responsibility for and fulfill these responsibilities meticulously for refugees, asylum seekers and immigrants to be able to rebuild their lives safely against serious dangers. Sharing responsibility for global problems is fair in the 21st century.

Welcoming people from other countries might empower host communities by making them more diverse and more flexible in a rapidly changing world. Some of the successful, impactful, and productive people in the field of arts, politics, and technology can be refugees, asylum seekers, or migrants. There are very successful people in the international community who have been given the opportunity to start a new life in another country and become a member of a new community.

In the 21st century, leaders, by showing sufficient political will, should produce and develop new projects to relocate people fleeing conflict and persecution in their countries.

Furthermore, the practice of other safe approaches should be implemented to enable refugees to start a new life. Providing the necessary financial support for refugee families to come to the country and granting them a study or work visa might be considered as an appropriate method for them to establish a new life.

States should not force anybody to return to a country where they might be subjected to human rights violations. Instead, states should ensure a safe place for refugees and asylum seekers, and migrants to live, a job, access to education, and health services.

Refugees, asylum seekers, and immigrants should be treated with dignity without being deprived of their freedom as stated in the United Nations

Universal Declaration of Human Rights. Under all the circumstances which require detention and retention, refugees, asylum seekers, and immigrants should be informed about their current rights as well as their fundamental rights. Their detention conditions should comply with international standards in terms of rights and freedoms.

Comprehensive programs should be prepared with the United Nations Member States and the United Nations High Commissioner for Refugees on the provision of social and legal assistance to refugees, asylum seekers and migrants. For this purpose, a valid and secure "country of origin information system" should be established. This system should be targeted to be structured as an "international joint system".

All these developments have revealed the necessity of preparing a multidimensional, original, up-to-date, original and rich content about refugees, asylum seekers and immigrants in the international community and presenting it to science.

This six volume book series is titled "Refugee Crisis in International Politics" are prepared with the aim of clarifying the above-mentioned issues and enriching the content, context, and depth to the field of science.

The role of the international organizations in formulation, development and evolution of refugee policies is the focus of the contributions in the third volume. We have eight chapters presented as follows: Doğan Şafak Polat "United Nations High Commissioner for Refugees and its Relations with the other United Nations' Organs"; Ebru Gür and Soyalp Tamçelik "Interagency Cooperation between UNHCR and ILO (International Labour Organization) on the Promotion of Refugees Right to Work"; Ebru Gür and Soyalp Tamçelik "Demographic Reports of UNHCR for Refugees"; İsmail Melih Baş "The Sustainable Development Goals (SDGs) and Migrants / Migration"; Dinçer Bayer "Refugee Policy of North Atlantic Treaty Organization (NATO)"; Adnan Seyaz "NATO and the Current Refugee Crisis Prospects and Challenges"; Furkan Yıldız "Refugee Policies of Council of Europe"; and Hazar Dördüncü "The Impact of International Trade Organizations on the Refugee Crisis".

We would like to thank all the contributing and researching colleagues who supported us with their research and findings.

We would like to express our gratitude to Prof. Dr. İbrahim Sirkeci who made the publication of "Refugee Crisis in International Politics" possible.

Special thanks should be given to the staff of Transnational Press London (TPLondon) for their valuable guidance and technical support on this process, for preparing our books for publication, and for designing the covers.

We sincerely hope that the work will be useful and useful to the world of science.

Hasret Çomak, Burak Şakir Şeker, Mehlika Özlem Ultan, Yaprak Civelek, Çağla Arslan Bozkuş

ISTANBUL, MARCH / 2021

CHAPTER 1

UNITED NATIONS HIGH COMMISSIONER FOR REFUGEES AND ITS RELATIONS WITH THE OTHER UNITED NATIONS' ORGANS

Doğan Şafak Polat[*]

Introduction

Since its establishment on December 14, 1950, after World War II, the United Nations (UN) High Commissioner for Refugees (UNHCR) has helped millions of people who have fled or lost their homes.[1] This organization aims to save lives, secure rights and create a sustainable future for refugees, forcibly displaced communities and stateless people.[2] It advocates that everyone in their country who has escaped abuse, oppression, war or catastrophe has the right to seek asylum and reach safe refuge.[3] Both the UNHCR Statute and the 1951 Convention and the 1967 Protocol gave UNHCR responsibility to oversee the governmental implementation of international refugee law instruments. It describes the term "refugee" and sets out the rights of refugees and the legal responsibilities of 149 State parties to care for them. In a way, it could be said that UNHCR served as the "guardian" of the 1951 Convention and the 1967 Protocol. States are required to work with UNHCR under the law to ensure that the rights of refugees are respected and secured.[4]

The UNHCR Office has been active since 1 January 1951, pursuant to UN General Assembly (GA) Resolution 319 (IV).[5] The GA renewed UNHCR's mandate every three years until 2003. However, with the GA

[*] Assoc. Prof. Dr., Istanbul Arel University, Faculty of Economics and Administrative Sciences, Department of International Relations, Istanbul, Turkey. E-mail: doganpolat@arel.edu.tr ORCID ID https://orcid.org/0000-0003-0786-1789
[1] United Nations GA Resolution 429(V) of 14 December 1950, retrieved from http://www.unhcr.org/refworld/docid/3b00f08a27.html (Access 08.09.2020).
[2] At least **79.5 million** people have been forced to leave their homes world wide. Almost **26 million refugees** are among them, about half of who mare under the age of 18. Millions of stateless citizens have also been denied nationality and lackaccess to the basic rights such as education, healthcare, work and freedom of movement. The role of the UNHCR is more critical than ever at a time when **1 percent of the world's population has left their homes** due to the war or persecution. See https://www.unhcr.org/figures-at-a-glance.html (Access 10.09.2020).
[3] UNHCR, "About Us", https://www.unhcr.org/about-us.html (Access 11.09.2020).
[4] Convention and Protocol Relating to The Status of Refugees, available at https://www.unhcr.org/3b66c2aa10
[5] Statute of the Office of the UNHCR, retrieved from https://www.unhcr.org/4d944e589.pdf (Access 11.09.2020).

Decision No. 58/153 in 2003, UNHCR's temporary mandate was extended until "the refugee problem is resolved."[6] UNHCR's mandate does not cover refugees who obtained assistance at the time of the establishment of the UNHCR Office from another UN agency. Until today, the role of UNHCR in protecting refugees has undergone significant changes and its structure has changed accordingly. In this context, its mandate for non-refugees such as stateless persons, internally displaced persons (IDPs) and returnees has been expanded.

In addition to providing technical and organizational assistance, UNHCR also provides adequate assistance for the basic needs of refugees such as housing, food, water, sanitation, medical care and education.[7] It also plays a crucial role in deciding the status and registration of refugees who do not have sufficient capability to take on these missions on their own in the host countries.

UNHCR, a program managed by the UN GA and the UN Economic and Social Council (ECOSOC), cooperates with many other UN programs and institutions to protect the rights of refugees in a better way. UNHCR has 17,324 personnel, located in 135 countries, mostly on the field.[8] This worldwide operation has become a highly complex activity such as recruiting new people, ensuring their safety in dangerous situations, procuring medical supplies and aircraft leasing. Critical areas such as operations, protection, external relations, human resources, and finance are audited through various departments at headquarters in Geneva. Furthermore, there are a variety of ties between overseas offices and headquarters in regional offices. UNHCR develops bilateral cooperation with governments as well as international organizations and institutions on protection matters. Determining the status of refugees for the protection and making a Memorandum of Understanding (MoU) between countries in the region are the most vital tasks undertaken by UNHCR. UNHCR also ensures inter-agency coordination to find adequate responses to large-scale refugee flows.

This article consists of three parts. In the first part, background information on UNHCR is provided. In the second part, UNHCR's structure, culture and mandate are explained briefly. In the last part, the article identifies UNHCR's relations with the other UN's organs.

---

[6] UN GAResolution 58/153 (Implementingactionsproposed by the UNHCR to strengthen the capacity of his Office to carry out its mandate), retrieved from https://www.iom.int/jahia/webdav/shared/shared/mainsite/policy_and_research/un/58/A_RES_58_153_en.pdf (Access 11.09.2020).

[7] UNHCR, 2017, A Guide to International Refugee Protection and Building State Asylum Systems, p. 42, retrieved from http://www.unhcr.org/3d4aba564.html (Access 13.09.2020).

[8] UNHCR, "Governanceand Oversight", retrieved from https://www.unhcr.org/ governance.html (Access 13.09.2020).

Background information on UNHCR and its statute

Overall, the beginning of the international refugee protection regime goes back to the 20th century, when the first international legal joint initiative for refugee protection took place. Initial efforts were made by the League of Nations in the 1920s and 1930s.These initial initiatives concerned the flow of population resulting from the fall of the Austro-Hungarian, Ottoman and Russian Empires, and later from the revolution and civil war that took place in Russia. The League of Nations established the Office of the High Commissioner for Russian Refugees in 1921 to solve the problem of Russian refugees. High Commissioner Fridtjof Nansen has been tasked with ensuring employment opportunities and repatriation regulations for refugees.[9] The documents prepared in this process were later referred to as "Nansen passports", probably because of Nansen's efforts to provide ID and travel documents to refugees.[10] Vital Nansen Passports were not only a valid identity or travel document for refugees, but were also necessary for refugees to advance into their first countries of asylum.[11] Then Nansen's mandate was enhanced to the people displaced after the collapse of the Ottoman Empire, namely Armenians, Assyrians, Syriac-Chaldeans, Kurds, Syrians and Turks.[12] After Nansen's death in 1930, the Nansen International Refugees Office was established to resume focusing on relief work.

Various institutions were established during the League of Nations period (1921-1946) to fulfill some or all of the duties of the High Commissioner for Refugees. These institutions are "the Nansen International Office for Refugees (1931-1938), the Office of the High Commissioner for Refugees coming from Germany (1933-1938), the Office of the High Commissioner of the League of Nations for Refugees (1939-1946) and the Intergovern-mental Committee on Refugees (1938-1947)".[13] These institutions provided international protection to refugees on the basis of international legal instruments, which are generally concluded in the context of the League of Nations. With the first Regulations made on 5 July 1922, 31 May 1924 and 12 May 1926, a definition of Russian and Armenian refugees was provided and primarily covered subjects such as "identity documents" essential for refugees. States parties assumed important responsibilities on behalf of Russian, Armenian and assimilated refugees for the first time in the context

---

[9] UNHCR, 2005, An Introduction to International Protection: Protecting Persons of Concern to UNHCR, p.5, retrievedfromhttps://www.unhcr.org/publications/legal/3ae6bd5a0/self-study-module-1-introduction-international-protection-protecting-persons.html (Access 13.09.2020).
[10] Shauna Labman, "Looking Back, Moving Forward: The History and Future of Refugee Protection", **Chicago-Kent Journal of International and Comparative Law**, Vol. 10, No.1, 2010, p. 3.
[11] James C. Hathaway, **The Rights of Refugeesunder International Law**, Cambridge: Cambridge University Press, 2005, p. 84.
[12] Gilbert Jaeger, "On the History of the International Protection of Refugees", **International Review of theRed Cross**, Vol. 83, No. 843, 2001, p. 729.
[13] Ibid.

of the Convention Relating to the Status of International Refugees of 28 October 1933.Administrative measures related to the issuance of "Nansen certificates" covered issues such as *refoulement*, legal issues, working conditions, industrial accidents, welfare and assistance, education, financial regime and reciprocity exemption, and also led to the "establishment of committees for refugees."

The 1933 Convention, which was ratified by nine States, including France and the United Kingdom, the most important states of the period, is a turning point in the protection of refugees and a model for the 1951 Convention. However, the United Kingdom did not accept the second paragraph of Article 3. Nevertheless, thanks to this Convention, the principle of non-refoulement gained the status of international treaty law. Two agreements to provide protection to refugees from Germany should also be mentioned: the Provisional Regulation on the Status of Refugees from Germany, signed in Geneva on 4 July 1936,[14] and the Convention Relating to the Legal Status of Refugees from Germany signed in Geneva on February 10, 1938.[15] Similarly, the 1938 Convention was created on the basis of the 1933 Convention. An Additional Protocol to the treaties opened for signature in Geneva on 14 September 1939 expanded these treaties to contain refugees from Austria.[16] Since refugees from Germany do not have the right to receive a Nansen certificate, a separate identity document has been provided with these treaties. The 1936 Provisional Regulation and the 1938 Convention did not mention the term refoulement, and their provisions on asylum are weaker than those of the 1933 Convention. It was also reported that refugees could be "returned to the Reich border" in some extreme circumstances. The resolution adopted by the Intergovernmental Committee on Refugees (IGCR) in Evian on 14 July 1938 to define its functions was another important international legal instrument put forward at that time.[17] The Evian meeting, with the contributions of President Franklin Roosevelt, was held outside the official system of the League of Nations "to facilitate the involuntary immigration from Germany (including Austria)."The next significant step in international protection was the establishment of the International Organization for Refugees (IRO).It was founded on 15 December 1946 by the UN GA Resolution 62 (I).It originally worked as the Preparatory Commission for the IRO from July 14, 1947 to August 20, 1948, and then worked as a full IRO from August 1948 until it was dissolved on February 28 1952.Although

---

[14] League of Nations, Treaty Series, Vol. CLXXI, No. 3952, retrieved from https://www.refworld.org/docid/3dd8d0ae4.html (Access 14.09.2020).
[15] League of Nations, Treaty Series, Vol. CXCII, No. 4461, p. 59, retrieved from https://www.refworld.org/docid/3dd8d12a4.html (Access 14.09.2020).
[16] League of Nations, Treaty Series,Vol. CSCVIII, No. 4634, p. 141, retrieved from https://www.refworld.org/docid/3dd8d1fb4.html (Access 14.09.2020).
[17] Gilbert Jaeger, "On theHistory of the International Protection of Refugees", **International Review of the Red Cross**, Vol. 83, No. 843, 2001, pp. 676-677.

Initially, the IRO was aimed to finish its operational activities by June 30, 1950, the refugee problem proved impossible to resolve by that date.[18]

The ECOSOC recognized the need to establish, at a suitable time, an international permanent mechanism to ensure the protection of stateless persons. For this reason it appointed an ad hoc Committee on Refugees and Stateless Persons on 8 August 1949.

In resolution 319 (IV) of 3 December 1949, based on Article 14 of the 1948 Universal Declaration of Human Rights, as of 1 January 1951 the UN GA determined to found a High Commissioner's Office for Refugees.

The Statute of the UNHCR was adopted by the GA as an Annex to Resolution 428 (V) on 14 December 1950.[19]In this Resolution, which is repeated on page 6, The GA also urged Governments to work together with the High Commissioner in the fulfillment of their duties regarding refugees falling under the Office's competence. In accordance with the Statute, the work of the High Commissioner, who has the responsibility to report to the GA every year, is humanitarian and social and completely non-political.[20] In accordance with paragraph 4 of the Statute, an Advisory Committee on Refugees was established by the ECOSOC[21] and was later re-established as the UN Refugee Fund (UNREF) Executive Committee.[22] Then it was replaced by the High Commissioner's Program Executive Committee in 1958.[23] Today the most important part of international refugee protection is the Office Statute.[24] UNHCR's function of supervision is outlined in its Statute, in the 1951 Convention, and in the 1967 Protocol. The convention entered into force on April 22, 1954. In accordance with Paragraph 8 of the Statute, UNHCR's functions in the protection of refugees are listed below:

(a) To encourage the conclusion and ratification of international conventions for the protection of refugees, to monitor their implementation and to propose changes to them;

(b) To encourage the adoption of any measure calculated to improve the situation of refugees and reduce the number of people in need of

---

[18] Ibid, p. 732.

[19] UN General Assembly, 1950, Statute of the Office of the UNHCR,p. 4, retrieved from https://www.refworld.org/docid/3ae6b3628.html (Access 15.09.2020).

[20] General Assembly Resolution 58/153 of 24 February 2004.

[21] Economic and Social Council Resolution 393 (XIII) B of 10 September 1951.

[22] Economic and Social Council Resolution 565 (XIX) of 31 March 1955 adopted pursuant to General Assembly Resolution 832 (IX) of 21 October 1954.

[23] General Assembly Resolution 1166 (XII) of 26 November 1957 and Economic and Social Council Resolution 672 (XXV) of 30 April 1958.

[24] UNHCR, "Statute of the Office of the UNHCR" https://www.unhcr.org/protection/basic/3b66c39e
1/statute-office-united-nations-high-commissioner-refugees.html (Access 15.09.2020).

protection through special agreements with governments;

(c) To support public and private programs to facilitate voluntary repatriation or assimilation into new national communities;

(d) To promote the entry into the territories of States of refugees, not except those in the most destitute categories;

(e) To strive to obtain permission for refugees to move their properties and in particular, those required to resettle them;

(f) To receive information from Governments on the number and conditions of refugees in their territories and the laws and regulations relating to them;

(g) To hold in close communication with the related governments and intergovernmental organizations;

(h) To establish contact with private organizations dealing with refugee concerns in such a way that they can think best;

(i) To make it easier for private organizations dealing with the protection of refugees to organize their efforts."[25]

With only one amendment to the 1951 Convention, geographical and temporal boundaries were abolished through the 1967 Protocol.[26]

In accordance with Article 35 (1) of the 1951 Convention and Article II of the 1967 Protocol, contracting states promise to work with the Office of the UNHCR or any other agency of the UN that may be succeed it, specifically, will ease its task of monitoring the application of the provisions [Convention and Protocol].[27] Pursuant to Article 35 (2) of the 1951 Convention, states are responsible for informing UNHCR about the laws, regulations and decrees they adopt in relation to refugees and the situation of refugees in their territories and the implementation of the Convention.

As an instrument of the post-Second World War, the 1951 Convention was initially constrained to just those fleeing events happening before 1 January 1951 and only in Europe. UNHCR won the Nobel Peace Prize in 1954 for its unique and exemplary work in Europe. The 1967 Protocol lifted

---

[25] UNHCR, "Statute of the Office of the UNHCR"https://www.unhcr. org/protection/basic/3b66c39e 1/statute-office-united-nations-high-commissioner-refugees.html(Access 21.09.2020).

[26] The Convention allowed States to make a statement when becoming members that the expression "events that occurred before 1 January 1951" was understood as "events that occurred in Europe"before that date. This geographic restriction was maintained by very few Nations and lost much of its significance with the adoption of the 1967 Protocol.The Protocol of 1967 is attached to UN GA Resolution 2198 (XXI) of 16 December 1967, retreived from http://www.unhcr.org/refworld/ docid/ 3b00f1cc50.html (Access 12.09.2020).

[27] UN General Assembly, Convention Relating to the Status of Refugees,1951, p. 176; 1967, p. 270, retrieved from https://www.refworld.org/docid/3be01b964.html (Access 23.09.2020).

the restrictions and there by gave universal context to the Convention. Since then, the 1967 Protocol has been assisted in different regions by refugee and subsidiary protection regimes, as well as by the progressive growth of international human rights law.

The 1951 Convention combines previously existing international refugee documents and provides the most detailed international codification of refugee rights.

Contrary to the previous international refugee documents referring to specific categories of refugees, a single definition of the term "refugee" was endorsed by the 1951 Convention in Article 1. The importance and difference of this definition is that it is about protecting people from political or other forms of persecution. Under the Convention, a "refugee" is a person who fails or does not want to return to his/her country of origin for fear of persecution because of his/her political opinion, nationality, religion, race or membership of a particular social group.

The Convention is an instrument focused on status and rights, and a variety of universal values, most notably non-discrimination, non-punishment and non-refoulement, also support it. For instance, the provisions of the Convention will be applied regardless of country of origin, religion or race.

Enhancements in international human rights law also strengthen the principle of non-discriminatory application of the Convention on the basis of gender, sexuality, disability, age or other prohibited grounds of discrimination. The Convention also lays down that, with some exceptions, refugees are not punished for their unlawful entry or residency. This acknowledges that seeking asylum may oblige refugees to breach immigration laws. Penalties prohibited may contain issues such as immigration charges, criminal offenses related to asylum seeking, or arbitrary detention solely focused on seeking asylum. More importantly, various provisions against the expulsion of refugees are included in the Convention. The non-refoulement principle is so universal that it is not possible to make any reservations or exceptions. It ensures that no one will involuntarily expel or return ("refouler") a refugee to an area where they fear threats to freedom or life.

The basic requirements for the treatment of refugees are laid down by the Convention; without regard to the more favorable treatment of states. These rights consist of provisions regarding access to primary education, courts, work and documents, including a refugee travel document in the form of a passport. However, the Convention does not apply to all persons who may somehow meet the refugee definition in Article 1. The Convention does not specifically apply to those who have serious reasons to believe that they have committed war crimes or violations of human rights, serious non-political crimes or acts contradictory to the aims and values of the UN. Refugees benefiting from the protection or assistance of a UN organization other than UNHCR are therefore not protected by the Convention. The Convention shall also not extend to refugees who are equal in status to citizens of their country of asylum.

In addition to expanding the definition of refugee, the Protocol requires States to comply with the material provisions of the 1951 Convention to all persons falling within the scope of the refugee definition in Article 1, without any date limitation. Although related in some way to the Convention, the Protocol is an independent document and accession is not confined to States which are party to the Convention.

UNHCR has a special function under the Convention and Protocol. States undertake to collaborate with UNHCR in the fulfillment of the operations contained in the 1950 Statute and outlined in a number of other GA Resolutions, and in particular to facilitate its task of overseeing the implementation of these instruments. According to its Statute, UNHCR is tasked with, among other tasks, to promote international instruments for the protection of refugees and to supervise their applications. The Convention and the Protocol constitute the foundational legal instruments that form the foundation of the work of the UNHCR.

149 State parties to one or both of the Convention and Protocol have defined the term "refugee" and identified the rights of refugees and the legal responsibilities of States to protect them. The fundamental part is the non-refoulement principle, arguing that a refugee should not be returned to a country where he or she faces serious threats to his life or freedom. This is now recognized as a rule of customary international law. The fundamental importance and enduring significance of the Convention are commonly accepted, as are the Protocol. In 2001, a Declaration was issued by the States Parties reaffirming their adherence to the 1951 Convention and the Protocol of 1967, and recognizing in particular the incorporation of the fundamental principle of non-refoulement in customary international law.[28] Nevertheless, the GA has also frequently encouraged States to be parties to these documents.

UNHCR's structure and mandate

In the years since its foundation, the international context in which UNHCR has to operate has changed dramatically and the frameworks under

---

[28] Declaration of States parties to the 1951 Convention and/or its 1967 Protocol Relating to the Status of Refugees, Ministerial Meeting of States Parties, Geneva, Switzerland, 12-13 December 2001, UN Doc. HCR/MMSP/2001/09, 16 January 2002. The Declaration was welcomed by the UN General Assembly in resolution A/RES/57/187, para. 4, adopted on 18 December 2001.

which UNHCR is based and the challenges faced by the organization need to be recognized. The international system has historically been dominated by states where sovereignty is the pillar of power and authority. The growing number of non-state actors and the significance of their position in world politics have introduced new aspects to humanitarian aid. Communication and coordination with local networks and different external actors are essential to the survival of the UNHCR because when working to accomplish its mandate, it must respond to local political concerns, desires and needs. While member states may provide a specific task or mandate, how it is interpreted, effective and implemented in the field depends on the communication and coordination of the organization. It is important to consider the constraints it faces within the UN framework, its internal culture and the conflicts within its mandate in order to examine UNHCR operations using "autonomy strategies."

Throughout history, refugees have been a constant, but no structured organizational framework was developed until the twentieth century. After World War II, European countries were filled with large numbers of displaced persons and refugees.[29]

Following several precedents, UNHCR was founded by the GA in 1950 and its Statute[30] gives the organization its mandate focusing on two roles: providing protection for refugees and resolving their plight. The Office was however, granted little accountability, little autonomy, a provisional mandate (renewable by the GA) and was resource-dependent on the member states.

UNHCR is managed by UN GA and ECOSOC. Member states have established mechanisms and procedures to limit UNHCR's mandate, autonomous capability and actions. First the member states set up the Executive Committee of the High Commissioner's Program (ExCom), an executive and advisory mechanism that approves the programs and budgets of the UNHCR, draws conclusions on international refugee protection policy issues and directs the internal work and priorities of the UNHCR. ExCom membership, appointed by the GA, is open to member states pending the election process. In order to continue its work between plenary sessions, the Ex Com's Standing Committee meets several times a year. A Standing Committee (see A/AC.96/860) was formed by ExCom in October 1995 to replace subcommittees on foreign security and administrative and financial

---

[29] As defined by the 1951 Convention and its Protocol of 1967, a refugee"is any person who, due to a well-founded fear of persecution on grounds of ethnicity, religion, nationality, membership of a particular social group or political opinion, is outside the country of his or her nationality and is unable or unwilling to take advantage of that country's security because of such fear; or who, having no nationality and being outside the country of his for her habitual residence, is unable or unwilling to return to it because of such fear."

[30] 1950 Statute of the Office of the UNHCR.

issues. The Chairman of the Executive Committee and the Vice-Presidents share the Standing Committee Chairmanship. The Standing Committee meets three times a year.

After its establishment in 1958, membership has grown and many strong donor countries have tried to retain their influential influence on policy issues and goals. Second, the member states granted the organization a temporary mandate[31] that only the GA could renew and expand the operations. Since its formation, the GA has been instrumental in enhancing the reach and dimension of the work of the UNHCR through the use of its authority to issue policy directives. Third, although the UNHCR operates under the mandate of the GA and is capable of fulfilling its mandate under the auspices of the UN, it essentially relies on the mandate and funding of the Member States. The financial structure of the organization specifies that only administrative expenditure from the UN budget would be funded and that any other expenditure relating to the Office's operations should be financed by voluntary donations (initially only from member states). Although UNHCR was founded with certain humanitarian ideas, donor states' support also depended on how states perceived the eligibility of the Office and particular refugee conditions in their national interests.[32] Material limitations and donor preferences have affected many of UNHCR's policies and practices; however the group found ways to expand its importance and impact by using "autonomy strategies."

Historically, the UNHCR's responsibilities to protect and pursue solutions have functioned as a restraint on the organization. Although there are many reasons why her two-part mandate could limit her actions, two of them are explicitly important to this research. First, while the Law specifies that "the High Commissioner's work would be of a strictly non-political nature,"[33] the Office's work is also political in nature and needs political solutions. In addition, to fulfill its mandate, the UNHCR has been tasked with serving as the head of the international refugee regime.[34] Although this allows the organization to approach governments about its treatment of

---

[31] Limited extensions were issued by the UNHCR for over fifty years until recently. The GA abolished temporary restrictions on the Office in 2003 and guaranteed the life of UNHCR until the refugee issue is solved with great persuasion from High Commissioner Lubbers (2001-2005), acknowledging the hampering effects of providing a temporary mandate.

[32] Gil Loescher, **The UNHCR and World Politics: A Perilous Path**, Oxford: Oxford University Press, 2001.

[33] 1950 Statute of the Office of the UNHCR para. 2.

[34] A collection of interstate agreements and practices that specify the obligations of states to refugees are included in the global refugee regime. See Gil Loescher, Betts, A. And Milner J., **UNHCR: The Politics and Practice of Refugee Protection into the Twenty-first Century**, London: Routledge, 2008, p. 2. The 1951 Convention (and its Protocol of 1967) is at the core of the regime that identifies refugees and decides those who are eligible for refugee status and their rights. The 1951 Conventional so specifically determines UNHCR's oversight duty for its implementation.

refugees,[35] if it fails to fulfill its treaty commitments, it does not allow the UNHCR to take action against a state. A state's right to modify its conduct in violation of the 1951 convention is limited. In the expectation that it can alter the way the state behaves with the embarrassment and pressure of the people, it may draw attention to these violations; but it must proceed with caution. The UNHCR seeks permission from the host government to carry out its mission in a specific country and should leave when told to do so. Secondly, the mandate of the UNHCR does not grant operational independence to the organization. To introduce financial assistance programs and to finalize refugee procedures, such as repatriation and resettlement, the UNHCR should rely on other institutions and organizations. The host government has the ultimate authority in this situation, as the institutions and organizations that operate the programs of the UNHCR must also receive permission.[36] "Therefore the efforts of UNHCR are constrained by the tension between the duty to protect qualified people with humanitarian needs and the legal, administrative and political reality that it cannot be replaced by governments that support or use its services as an organization."[37]

When examining the structure of UNHCR; "UNHCR, with its unique culture and value system, is an individual represented by the High Commissioner and the bureaucracy because it is unique within the UN system."[38] The position of leadership is significant in an organization like UNHCR. UNHCR leadership involves legal, diplomatic, programmatic and public relations roles, all of which rely on the organization's expertise.[39] Furthermore, it is not possible to consider the internal structure and management of a multinational bureaucracy to be distinct from its external environment. Over time, the organizational structure of UNHCR has grown, extending its activities that influence the overall strategy of the organization.[40] There are also internal levels of autonomy inherent in a decentralized and space-oriented International Organization, such as UNHCR, that affect the organization's activities.

UNHCR set out with a small staff and budget as a Geneva-based organization. As of 31 May 2020, increasing the size and scope of its operations, UNHCR had reached 17,324 staff in 135 countries, of which approximately 90% are on the ground.[41] With an informal annual budget of

---

[35] Leon Gordenker, 1988, p. 276.
[36] Leon Gordenker, 1988, p. 281.
[37] Ibid.
[38] Gil Loescher et al., 2008, p. 74.
[39] Leon Gordenker, 1988, p. 289.
[40] Michael Barnettand Martha Finnemore **Rules forthe World: International Organisations in Global Politics**, New York: Cornell University Press, 2004.
[41] UNHCR, "How is UNHCR funded", https://www.unhcr.org/figures-at-a-glance.html(Access 24.09.2020).

US $ 300,000, UNHCR began its operations in 1950. However as their company and scale have increased, so have the costs as well. Its annual budget rose to over $1 billion in the early 1990s, and its budget rose dramatically to $8.6 billion a year in 2019.[42] This growth in the company has created and modified departments and divisions.

Approximately one-third of UNHCR staff is based at headquarters in Geneva and two-thirds on land around the world. Regional and country offices responsible for the enforcement of the Central Security and Assistance Directives oversee operations in the region.[43] This style of decentralized approach to action is often left open both in regional and country offices and in the field to interpretation by staff.

The organizational culture and action are influenced by staff stresses related to conflicts between headquarters and field offices, regular rotation, management difficulties, and the consequences of working in a crisis environment.[44] On the ground, by communicating with different parties, negotiating with government officials and introducing a range of initiatives, UNHCR staff can work to enforce global policy at the local level; this makes room for autonomous action. Different governance systems in different countries take into account the decentralized existence of the activities of UNHCR and the evolving context of operations in the sector.[45] In most cases, in the sense of the local position and circumstance, officials in the field believe they have the right to interpret. When conceived as local regimes that are part of but distinct from the international refugee regime, these organizational networks are active in policy execution create and are influenced by

"(1) the essence of their processes and relationships in decision - making;

(2) principles of norm-compliance, whereover time independent, partly shared understandings of what is most relevant among the various tasks to be performed[sic] are established and what constitutes success or failure;

(3) Practices: Organizational networks on the ground often form results by influencing the relative impact of various organizations or actors."[46]

In the UNHCR situation, it is argued that field offices are not only simple policy or guidance structures, but also autonomous actors with complex and critical diplomatic positions. The policy guidelines and activities of UNHCR

[42] Ibid.
[43] Gil Loescher et al., 2008, p.82.
[44] Gil Loescher et al., 2008.
[45] Gil Loescher et al., 2008, p.83.
[46] Anna Barbara Schmidt, **From Global Prescription to Local Treatment – the international refugee regime in Tanzania and Uganda**, PhD thesis, Department of Political, Science, University of California, Berkeley, 2006.

at headquarters can be prioritized, interpreted and enforced in various ways at ground level. Accountability is important for a humanitarian organization such as UNHCR as it is a way of ensuring more efficient security of rights, allowing people the opportunity to share their opinions on the activities of UNHCR and pursue recourse for abuses.[47] However there are insufficient and scarce institutional accountability mechanisms to keep UNHCR externally reviewed and hold it responsible for its actions.

UNHCR's lack of accountability and growing authority pose concerns about how the Office will be kept accountable for organizational errors, misuse of control, or behave in a manner that jeopardizes the refugees it is responsible for.[48] While there is little transparency inside UNHCR, this does not mean that the company violates the rights of those it serves to safeguard. However it is important to note that when analyzing accountability for UNHCR, the Bureau is divided between the UN, donor states, as well as many organizations or entities that may affect or be impacted by an organization's actions. The GA's Resolutions on the persons concerned extended the personal mandate of UNHCR to include internally displaced persons (IDPs), stateless persons, repatriated refugees and the war-affected population beyond refugees and asylum seekers.[49] Many UNHCR activities that are accountable to several stakeholders represent the needs of one or the other rather than the other and have the potential for those stakeholders to be negative or harmful.

In short, the capacity of the UNHCR to fulfill its role must be measured in relation to its place within the context of the UN, the political nature of its work and the sophistication of its bureaucratic culture. The acts of the UNHCR were limited by the UN structure, donor states, and UNHCR corporate culture, but the organization showed that this was not a submissive process by which states could function. Although the UNHCR is limited by governments, the idea that it is a passive mechanism without an autonomous purpose alone is not justified by empirical evidence from the past half-century. It seems clear that the autonomy and authority of UNHCR in world politics has evolved over time, and the Bureau, with its independent interests and capabilities, has become a target-oriented player in its own right.[50] As mentioned, when trying to strike a balance between protecting refugees and

---

[47] Mark Pallis, "The Operation of UNHCR'sAccountability Mechanism'", **Working Paper 12**, New York: New York University Institute for International Law and Justice,
http://www.law.nyu.edu/journals/jilp/issues/37/NYI406_Pallis.pdf (Access 28.09.2020).
[48] Gil Loescher et al., 2008, p.74.
[49] Erin D. Mooney, "In-country Protection: Out of Bounds for UNHCR?", in Frances Nicholson and Patrick Twomey(eds*), **Refugee Rights and Realities: Evolving International Concepts and Regimes**, Cambridge: Cambridge University Press, 1999.
[50] Gil Loescher, **The UNHCR and World Politics: A PerilousPath**, Oxford: Oxford University Press, 2001, p. 6.

the sovereign desires and interests of states, the UNHCR finds itself on a "dangerous path." As demonstrated by the basis of the mandate of the UNHCR, the overview of some of the internal aspects of the UNHCR has delegated control from the member states that have formed it. The UNHCR has delegated authority, in particular, from the member states that have formed it. The UNHCR has delegated authority, in particular, from the member states that formed it. Based on its position as the protector and spreader of international refugee law and principles, it has moral authority and has expertise based on deep expertise and experience in refugee movements and refugee law and related matters.[51]

It is possible to examine the shifting context in which the organization finds itself in the 2020s, with the foundation of the UNHCR authority, the limitations of the UN framework, the dynamics of the bureaucratic community, and the contradictions within its mandate.

UNHCR's relations with the other UN's organs

Unquestionably, forced migration and statelessness are problems of importance to the UN. In response to these challenges, after World War II, UNHCR and its office were founded as the global refugee agency. UNHCR is operated by UN GA and ECOSOC. The High Commissioner's mandate was born in 1950 by the UN GA, from the experience of the numerous international refugee organizations that existed during the interwar era. The GA's aim was to ensure that the High Commissioner, assisted by his Office, *"would enjoy a special status within the UN... possessing the degree of independence and prestige that would appear to be necessary for the effective performance of his duties."* The High Commissioner is directly elected by the GA, works annually under her mandate and reports to her.[52] The functions and responsibilities laid down in the Law of the Office are those of the High Commissioner, from whom special authority is obtained.

Legally, by Resolution 319 A(IV) of 3 December 1949, the High Commissioner and his Office constitute a multilateral, intergovernmental body constituted by GA as its affiliated organ, and by Resolution 14, by its Statute of 428(V) of December 1950 (Annex). The Statute stipulates that "acting under the GA's mandate, the High Commissioner will take on the task of ensuring international security... and seeking permanent solutions to the refugee crisis."[53]

The Statute is not however, the sole source of authority for the powers of

---

[51] Gil Loescher et al., 2008, p.19.
[52] Para. 11 of the Statute of the Office of the High Commissioner for Refugees, as revised by General Assembly (GA) res. 58/153, 22 December 2003.
[53] Para. 1 of the Statute.

the High Commissioner and his office. The further implementation of its roles and operations is provided for in Paragraph 9 of the Law.[54] It is the High Commissioner who is responsible for UNHCR administration and oversight. With the aid of a Deputy High Commissioner and the Deputy High Commissioner for Security and Procedures, he or she guides the work of the UNHCR. GA and, to some degree, ECOSOC have further established the mandate since 1950. The powers of the High Commissioner and his office have also been expanded by "goodwill" agreements from time to time.

Other tasks can include "at the request of the Secretary General, where the Office has unique expertise and experience," intervention and involvement in the UN humanitarian effort. The Chief Inspector's Office provides impartial assurance and oversight of the activities and operations of the UNHCR to the High Commissioner. It ensures the credibility and reliability of the programs and operations of UNHCR. Via internal audits, inquiries and other oversight consultancy services, it also discourages fraud and abuse.

In 2003, the GA expanded the mandate of UNHCR "until the refugee problem is resolved." The High Commissioner reports annually on the work of UNHCR to the ECOSOC and the GA. One of the six major UN GA committees is the Third Committee of the UN GA (also known as the Social, Humanitarian and Cultural Committee or SOCHUM or C3). It focuses on human rights, humanitarian affairs and social issues. Each year the Third Committee meets in early October and aims to complete its work by the end of November. Both 193 UN member states are eligible to join. A considerable part of the work of the Committee will concentrate on the review of human rights issues, including reports on the particular procedures defined in 2006 by the Human Rights Council. It reports concerns and humanitarian issues concerning refugees, returnees and displaced persons to the UNHCR.[55]

The UN GA hosted the UN Summit on Refugees and Migrants on September 19, 2016, a high-level summit focused specifically on refugee and migrant movements to put together countries for a more humane and organized approach.[56] It was attended by the representatives of the UN High Commissioner for Human Rights, the UN Department for Gender Equality

---

[54] Para. 9 of the Statute stipulatesth at the High Commissioner should engage in such additional activities as the GA may determine, subject t resources available. Furthermore, the High Commissioner is required to follow policy directives given to him by the GA orthe ECOSOC, pursuant to para. 3 of the Statute.

[55] See "Resolution adopted by the General Assembly on 19 December 2017", https://www.unhcr.org/excom/bgares/5acdb5887/assistance-refugees-returnees-displaced-persons-africa-resolution-adopted.html?query=un%20security%20council(Access 16.10.2020).

[56] UNHCR, "History of UNHCR", https://www.unhcr.org/pages/49c3646cbc.html(Access 16.10.2020).

and Women's Empowerment, the UN Office on Drugs and Crime and the World Bank. At the summit, the key factors and motivations for migration and the need for global cooperation were addressed. The UN has announced a set of principles as a result of this summit that urge the international community to develop the momentum set by the 2016 adoption of the New York Declaration of Refugees and Immigrants.[57]

The 20 draft principles concentrate explicitly on human rights; non-discrimination; rescue and assistance; access to justice; border governance; reimbursement; violence; custody; family union; immigrant children; immigrant women; right to health; adequate standard of living; smooth work; right to education; right to information; monitoring and accountability; immigrant human rights defenders; data; and intellectual property rights.[58] UNHCR collaborated with the UN Food and Agriculture Organization in Tehran on 28 September 2016 to initiate a Response Plan for Afghan Refugees. FAO highlighted FAO's contribution to the SSAR objectives for livelihood-related programs, including livestock and fisheries initiatives and nutrition projects in schools in Iran. The FAO and UNHCR are committed to increasing access to livelihoods for refugees and reducing dependency on humanitarian assistance. A collaborative livelihood strategy for South Sudan has recently been launched, which aims to resolve this issue with a clearly established action plan. In refugee-hosting areas throughout the world, the policy targets both refugees (70 percent) and local communities (30 percent).[59]

UNHCR provides Syrian refugees with life-saving humanitarian aid, providing the most vulnerable with cash for medicine and food, stoves and heating fuel, tent insulation, warm blankets and winter clothes. UNHCR provides shelter kits and non-food products for those who have been displaced but remain in Syria, as well as security services and psychosocial help.[60] UNHCR joined forces with other UN humanitarian and development agencies in early 2017, with Syria's war going into its seventh year and with no end to the fighting in sight, to appeal for US$8 billion in crucial new funding to aid millions of people in Syria and throughout the country.[61] The

---

[57] UN, "71/1. New York Declaration for Refugees and Migrants",Resolution adopted by the General Assembly on 19 September 2016, https://www.un.org/en/ga/search/view_doc.asp?symbol=A/RES/71/1(Access 17.10.2020).
[58] UN News, "UN official unveils draft principles on protecting humanrights of refugees and migrants",20 September 2016, https://news.un.org/en/story/2016/09/539582-un-official-unveils-draft-principles-protecting-human-rights-refugees-and#.V-xRGvCLQ2w(Access 17.10.2020).
[59] FAO Regional Office for Africa, "UNHCR and FAO help vulnerable refugees and South Sudanese families strengthen their food security", http://www.fao.org/africa/news/detail-news/en/c/417501/ (Access 20.10.2020).
[60] **13.1 million** people in need in Syria, **6.6 million** internally displaced persons, **2.98 million** people in hard-to-reach and besieged areas. See UNHCR, "Syria Emergency", https://www.unhcr.org/syria-emergency.html (Access 20.10.2020).
[61] UNHCR, "History of UNHCR", https://www.unhcr.org/pages/49c3646cbc.html (Access

Regional Refugee and Resilience Plan (3RP), for 2018-2019, is the first component of the appeal. It calls for US$4.4 billion, led by the UNHCR, to help more than 5 million refugees in neighboring countries and some four million people in their host communities. The second factor is the Syria Humanitarian Response Plan 2017, which seeks approximately US$3.2 billion to provide 13.5 million people within Syria with humanitarian assistance and security.[62]

UNHCR is regarded as one of the most involved contributors of the UN to the frameworks for human rights.[63] The States in the Human Rights Council and the Universal Periodic Review (UPR) context,[64] as well as the experts of the Treaty Bodies and Special Procedures Mandate Holders, highly appreciate their direct knowledge of human rights issues on the ground. The comprehensive field network not only places the UNHCR in a unique position to collect and provide information on persons engaging with the UN human rights process, but also tracks and promotes the implementation of its findings with a view to achieving the required improvements in the protection environment, the national practices of legislation affecting persons within its jurisdiction.[65]

As humanitarian crises have become more complex, both the number and form of organizations with which UNHCR works have been increased. It works closely with or is approaching sister UN agencies whose work has been completed. The World Food Programme (WFP), the UN Children's Fund (UNICEF), the World Health Organization (WHO the UN Development Programme (UNDP), the Office for the Management of Humanitarian Affairs (OCHA), the UN High Commissioner for Human Rights (OHCHR) and the Joint UN Programme on HIV/AIDS are among the most important agencies (UNAIDS).

Via the "Delivering as One" project, UNHCR is committed to working more closely with other organizations, seeking to improve UN collaborative action in the areas of sustainability, humanitarian aid and the environment.

22.10.2020).

[62] Ibid.

[63] UNHCR, "Human Rights Engagement Strategy, The Case For Inclusion 2020-2023", https://www.unhcr.org/ protection/operations/5fb681264/unhcrs-human-rights-engagement-strategy-2020-2023.html?query=un%20 security%20council (Access 25.10.2020).

[64] The UPR is a special Human Rights Council (HRC) processaimed at **improving the human rights situation on the ground** in each of the 193 Member States of the UN. The human rights situation of all UN member states is checked every 5 years under this framework. During three Working Group sessions devoted to 14 States each, 42 States are reviewed each year. In January/February, May/June and October/November, these three sessions are commonly held. The outcome of each review is expressed in the Working Group Final Report, which lists the **recommendations** that will have to be adopted by the State under review (SuR) before the next review.

[65] See "UNHCR's Engagement With National Human Rights Institutions", https://www.unhcr.org/ protection/operations/5f92a5604/guidance-unhcrs-engagement-national-human-rights-institutions. html?query=un%20 security%20council (Access 30.10.2020).

In addition, the so-called "cluster approach" to their emergency was embraced by displaced persons, IDP (internally displaced persons), where various organizations lead their field of expertise when working together to assist those in need. As well as camp coordination and management, UNHCR leads the way in protection and shelter needs.

On January 16, 2017, the UNHCR revealed its strategic course between 2017 and 2021.[66] Five key issues will be discussed by UNHCR: protection; emergency response and beyond; fostering inclusiveness and self-confidence, including the involvement of development actors; inspiring the people represented by UNHCR; and finding solutions. Efforts will be followed in these fields in a mutually supporting and coordinated manner.

Although there are a range of particular activities aimed at securing rights and meeting needs, all fields of action will also be directed and assisted by protection. Working at the implementation level in various areas would contribute to our planning and operations. It will also guide our efforts to establish holistic responses to the broad spectrum of refugee situations needed by the Refugees and Immigrants Declaration of New York. UNHCR will lead wherever it is expected and acceptable to achieve these objectives, but will also rely heavily on a number of broad and diverse collaborations to promote shared objectives in all areas of its work.

Conclusion

To support millions of Europeans who fled or lost their homes after the Second World War, the UNHCR office was established in 1950. In 1954, for its pioneering work in Europe, UNHCR received the Nobel Peace Prize. It didn't take long for us though, to face our next big emergency. There were 200,000 people who fled to neighboring Austria during the Hungarian Revolution in 1956. UNHCR led the resettlement efforts by identifying the Hungarians as "at first sight" refugees. The way humanitarian organizations deal with potential refugee crises was influenced by this uprising and its aftermath.

In the 1960s, Africa's decolonization provided the first of many refugee crises on this continent. Over the next two decades, it has supported displaced individuals in Asia and Latin America. In 1981, he was awarded the second Nobel Peace Prize for helping refugees across the globe. UNHCR is operated by UN GA and ECOSOC, respectively. The Executive Board of UNHCR approves the biennial activities of the department and the accompanying budget. These are addressed by the UN GA-appointed High Commissioner. The Program Executive Committee of the High

---

[66] UNHCR, "UNHCR's Strategic Directions 2017–2021", https://www.unhcr.org/excom/announce/5894558d4/unhcrs-strategic-directions-2017-2021.html (Access 10.11.2020).

Commissioner (ExCom) meets annually in Geneva to review and approve the programs and budget of the Organization, to advise on foreign security, and to address a number of other issues with UNHCR and intergovernmental and non-governmental partners.

UNHCR contributed to significant refugee crises in Africa, the Middle East and Asia at the beginning of the 21st century. We were also asked to use our skills to support more conflict-induced internally displaced people and to extend our role in helping stateless people. The 1951 Refugee Convention has been expanded by additional regional legal instruments in certain areas of the world, such as Africa and Latin America.

UNHCR employs 17,324 people as of 31 May 2020, about 90 percent of them in the industry. It operates in a total of 135 countries with its lowest annual budget of $300,000 in 1950 and its highest annual budget of $8.6 billion in 2019,[67] and 86% of its budget is almost entirely financed by voluntary donations, by governments and by the European Union. Three percent come from other intergovernmental organizations and joint financing mechanisms, while 10 percent, including the public, come from foundations, corporations and the private sector. It also receives a small operating expense subsidy (one percent) from the UN budget and accepts donations in kind including products such as tents, medicines and lorries.

Unfortunately, conflict, abuse, and sometimes extreme abuses of human rights have become a regular feature of the lives of millions of people worldwide. They were stuck in enclaves, or forced to leave their homes, surrounded by horrible conditions. Many have been cut off, living in long-term circumstances of uncertainty and turmoil, from their families and even from their countries. As security conditions deteriorate and access to defense becomes increasingly limited, more people are forced to travel by land or sea, as happens on every continent, in hopes of seeking safety further away. A concurrent approach to coping with both emergencies and development is proposed by UNHCR. Today, at the end of 2020, there are 79.5 million internally displaced people globally.[68] Almost 70 years later, UNHCR still continues to work tirelessly to help more than 50 million refugees around the world to protect and successfully resume their lives.

---

[67] UNHCR, "History of UNHCR", https://www.unhcr.org/history-of-unhcr.html (Access 17.11.2020).
[68] UNHCR, "Figures at a Glance", https://www.unhcr.org/figures-at-a-glance.html (Access 24.11.2020).

CHAPTER 2

INTERAGENCY COOPERATION BETWEEN THE UNHCR AND THE ILO ON THE PROMOTION OF REFUGEES RIGHT TO WORK

Ebru Gür* and Soyalp Tamçelik**

Introduction

This research is based on literature assessing international agencies' complex workings of power which illustrates how the norms and forms have been shaped around international government of borders. International Labour Organization (ILO) and United Nations High Commission on Refugees (UNHCR) are international organizations (IOs) exercise power by helping states in the promotion of refugees' right to work. The cooperation of autonomous and powerful actors ILO and UNHCR construct the social world with institutional practices in global politics. Over the last two decades interagency cooperation between ILO and UNHCR appear to create activities for economic reintegration with generalized rules and different models of political organizations.

In this research our constructivist perspective has been rooted in IOs as autonomous actors, challenging to international relation theories, tend to evaluate features of undesirable behaviors and unanticipated roles primarily in the context of Refugees. This approach makes our explanation constitutive and allows us to learn how bureaucracies are as a rational-legal authority constituted socially and politically by IOs. History of governmentality and neo-liberalism regarded as a sphere for normative valuation of ILO and UNHCR in empirical and ethical manner.

This essay contributes the cooperation between the Office of the United Nations High Commissioner for Refugees (UNHCR) and the International Labour Organization to address the challenges during development cooperation activities and government regulations for inter-community

* African Studies Ph.D. Student, Ankara Hacı Bayram Veli University, Department of International Relations, Turkey. E-mail: ebrugur1@outlook.com. ORCID ID: 0000-0003-4791-3598
** Prof. Dr.; Ankara Hacı Bayram Veli University, Faculty of Economics and Administrative Sciences, Head of International Relations Department, Turkey. E-mail: soyalp@hotmail.com. ORCID ID: 0000-0002-2092-8557

relations for protecting socio-economic rights of refugees, developing relevant legislative and policy framework in hosting countries. The first chapter will trace historical analysis of the establishment of the UNHCR and ILO. This will be followed by regarding correlation between refugees and process of migration policies to joint operational approaches in global politics. Through policy of ILO and UNHCR the state facilities prospered to robust international refugee framework. Finally, the second chapter will be presented by some narratives of UNHCR and ILO' interagency cooperation while defining norms and categories, they create internal bureaucratic pressures with international tasks and whether construct subtle mechanisms or subvert their self-professed goals.[1] Thus, with its distinctive complex schemes of governmentality practices embody with IOs regulations derives its empowerment from international law and agreements. In accordance with Barnett and Finnemore bureaucratic pathologies were consequences of *"social construction power"* that composed of five unexpected behaviors *"The irrationality of rationalization, Bureaucratic universalism, Normalization of Deviance, Organizational insulation and cultural contestation"*.[2] The consequences of this bureaucratic power have influence beyond their material resources and expertise knowledge on global politics. The initiative action of this constitutive process noted by Barnett and Finnemore as: *"IOs are powerful not so much... (as much as their material resources), ... use their authority to orient action and create social reality"* and also by interpreting information they converted it into knowledge which embodies their power to conduct set of normative values and norms. After establishing rules by international governmental organizations creates new classifications for actors and defines new missions for actors, and thereby models for transformation of governmentality in both social and political areas.

Historical Background of Intergovernmental Organizations: UNHCR and ILO

The ILO's reflections to states about migration policy since its foundation in 1919, set norms to facilitate understanding refugee identity as *"economic migrants"* in the economic perspective and to embody international tasks for refugee labour exchange in world politics. Indeed, IOs organizational matters as autonomous actors improve states to define responsibilities of mentioned authorities like generating a new regime. The ILO offices that had been opened in South Africa in 1926 were a specific focus on underlining the valuable contribution to refugee work. Despite the non-consensus over specifying the line between political refugee and poor migrants after World

---

[1] Michael Barnett and Martha Finnemore, **Rules for the World: International Organizations in Global Politics**, Ithaca, Cornell University Press, 2004, p. 8.
[2] ibid., pp. 7-40.

War II between the nation states, international actors generate onward settlements around legal protection issues. The interlocking effects of global economic crisis in 1929, states refused to make relevant laws and regulations for refugees seen as poor migrants. Despite prolonged European states debates over both the full extent of asylum and migrant structure which link to institutional behaviors regulates the tolerance of refugees. These pragmatic discourses showing the breakdown of refugees mobility contingency in the economic area which causes unemployment and poverty on the other hand. ILO was the first transitional agency from Cold War II to globalization with its regulatory functions which has been established in the new UN system. Conventions, Recommendations Declarations are subsystems of ILO's tripartite structure which was used to set international labour standards.[3] On 29 October 1919, the first International Labour Conference adopts social justice and perpetual peace declarations and helps the governments within international labour policy decisions.[4]

In the context of adequacies of Continental Europe' post-World War II pragmatic strategies intended to fulfill the gaps in mining, domestic and agricultural work have irrefutable connection with refugee protection establishment. While large scale of displaced person suffering from physical dislocation Nations Relief and Rehabilitation Association (UNRRA) provided a helping hand about repatriation after 1943. In other words, the current European economic and political problems have been solved by constructing fluid identities like refugee and migrants through 1920s and 1950s. The International Refugee Organization (IRO), subsystem of UNRRA, illustrates a context including only skilled refugees. IRO has moved away from establishing refugee claim according to their humanitarian needs by creating an independent migration category for refugees with exceptional rights. The dramatic blurred area for refugee and migrant identities between 1946 and 1952 in the terms of labour recruitment programmes began to shape with instruments like refugees right to settlement with Nanson Passport[5] in 1946. United Kingdom's (UKs) government negotiated programme, European Voluntary Worker (EVW), with Continental Europe's refugees requiring one-year work contracts could be regarded as permission for conditional migration. In the context of European refugee crisis administrative practices, reshaping migrant and refugee categories including the strategic use of the UKs state. Yet it was not only reformulating policies

---

[3] Francis Maupain, "New Foundation or New Facade? The ILO and the 2008 Declaration on Social Justice for a Fair Globalization", **The European Journal of International Law**, Vol. 20, No. 3, 2009, pp. 823-853.

[4] Conventions and Recommendations: 1919-1966: ILO, Geneva, 1966, pp. 1-18.

[5] The example of the changing dynamics in the "*international refugee protection regimes*" revealed the necessity for 800,000 Russian refugees to consolidate legal protection from restrictions in national territories to freedom of movement across international borders (Long, 2013, pp. 9-15).

on refugee populations, it was also an obvious working of power by using refugee migration as an instrument. IRO, '*temporary specialized agency*' of United Nations (UN), which was established in 1946 and its work was superseded by UNHCR in 1952.[6]

Engagement with International Refugee Policy

In November 1949, UNHCR was decided to establish in 1 January 1951 as a subsidiary agency of UN General Assembly with A/RES/319(IV) during 4th session which Resolutions and Decisions was adopted by General Assembly.[7] The refugee movement took the form of humanitarian and social as a '*non-political character*', seeking international protection for refugees with permanent solutions. This meant that UNHCR's mode of institution conducting governments for a legalistic approach about refugee matters rather than managing in operative aspects after transition from IRO regime. According to UN General Assembly A/RES/428(V), governments should cooperate with UNHCR in execution of measures to promote the admissions on their territories and improve the voluntary repatriation, thus have not coincide with the international community' aim to establish UNHCR in 1950.[8] The legal framework had been codified in 1951 firstly Convention on the Status of Refugees, Article 33, that transfer refugees' rights from political willingness to creation of humanitarian grounds for admission and refoulement.[9] UNHCR take the responsibility of imposing especially regional strategies relevant to establish rights of refugees with the 1951 Refugee Convention, international and regional instruments. To be eligible for this international protection, in Article 17, Wage-Earning Employment emphasis that:

"In any case, restrictive measures imposed on aliens or the employment of aliens for the protection of the national labour market shall not be applied to a refugee who was already exempt from them at the date of entry into force of this Convention for the Contracting State concerned, or who fulfils one of the following conditions:

(a) He has completed three years' residence in the country;

(b) He has a spouse possessing the nationality of the country of residence. A refugee may not invoke the benefits of this provision if he has abandoned

---

[6] United Nations, Treaty Series, Vol. 33, p. 302; Chapter III Privileges and Immunities, Diplomatic and Consular Relations, ETC, UNHCR, Geneva, 1949, p. 302.
[7] Mehmet Hasgüler ve Mehmet B. Uludağ, Devletlerarası ve Hükümet Dışı Uluslararası Örgütler, İstanbul, Alfa Yayınları, 2007, pp. 224-226.
[8] Statute of the Office of the United Nations High Commissioner for Refugees A/RES/428(V), UN General Assembly, Geneva, 1950, pp. 46-48.
[9] Katy Long, "When Refugees Stopped Being Migrants: Movement, Labour and Humanitarian Protection", Migration Studies. Vol. 1, No. 1, 2013, pp. 4-26.

his spouse;

(c) He has one or more children possessing the nationality of the country of residence".[10]

It is in this context that those drafting the 1951 Refugee Convention give equal opportunity refugees right to work and transfer models of policy for the integration of refugees as workers to societies and economies. UNHCR's regional bureaus contribute to how to solve the problem of governmentality by engaging uncertain strategies of regions at national- level which will have socio-economic impacts for refugees in the workplace. There was also Article 28, for the maintenance of the re-admission of the refugees with Convention Travel Documents which supplies refugee's mobility as migrants. Despite the aimed humanitarian needs both Convention and UNHCR haven't related with direct operations which were settled to protect refugee right to work or move. In other words, refugees' legal status has been focused on as a protector by UNHCR under international laws, but not implications in world politics. Thus, the commitments of 1951 Refugee Convention within a refugee framework rather than migrant workers which is mandated by application of the UN Convention on the Rights of All Migrant Workers and Their Families in 1990. Although ILO is apart from this convention, ILO has been attended meeting of *"the Committee on the Protection of the Rights of All Migrant Workers and Members of Their Families (CMV)"* to act advisory role in administration.[11] CMV has been entered into force on 1 July 2003, 33 state parties have been accepted this procedure on 1 October 2005 in which correlation between human rights and migrant workers, mostly this is issue also drew increasing attention on world policy.[12]

The committee held its first session in March 2004 to monitor how the provisions and measures adopted by State Parties. The boundaries between 1951 Refugee Convention and the UN Convention on the Rights of All Migrant Workers and Their Families in 1990 has been mentioned by Vincent Chetail.[13] As Chetail Notes, the Refugee law has been established on the gravitational force of human rights law, which can be regarded as *"complementary forms of protection"* with its limited regime. In other words, human rights law offers more protection than the refugee regime, since its human rights have a holistic view by supporting displacement efficiently.[14]

[10] **Convention and Protocol Relating to the Status of Refugees**, UN High Commissioner for Refugees, Geneva, 2010, pp. 1-56.
[11] See... https://www.ohchr.org/en/hrbodies/cmw/pages/cmwindex.aspx (Access: 18.08.2020).
[12] The International Convention on Migrant Workers and its Committee, Fact Sheet No. 24 (Rev.1), Office of the United Nations High Commissioner for Human Rights, Geneva, 2005, p. 1-66.
[13] Adele Garnier, "Arrested Development? UNHCR, ILO and the Refugees' Right to Work", **Canada's Journal on Refugees**, Vol. 30, No. 2, 2014, pp. 15-25.
[14] Colin Harvey, "Time for Reform? Refugees, Asylum-seekers and Protection Under International Human Rights Law", **Refugee Survey Quarterly**, Vol. 34, 2015, pp. 43-60.

UNHCR's constructed repatriation process to solve refugee crisis before 1980 is exemplification for the *"normalization of deviance"*, mechanism within bureaucratic pathologies has been determined by Barnett and Finnemore. The draft of UNHCR which is evidence for international refugee law focusing especially repatriation was resulted lowering barriers to increase involuntarily implications of States. ILO-UNHCR partnership in Kakuma and Dabaab refugee camp in order to enhance working skills is a good example for *"cultural contestation"* mechanism, which refers to developing norms without concerning historical experiences of regions in favor of different normative views. Because restrictive measures organized on the assumption of refugee rights and needs are the same around the world, but this certain approach to regional refugees ignores refugee settlement on the other side. UNHCR's humanitarian policies are more appropriate to illustrate with donor's line of funding, whereas it doesn't obtain a result among reconstruction and rehabilitation functions just as ILO. Addition to cultural contestation bureaucratic pathologies the nature of their collaboration also exemplifies organizational insulation mechanism. UNHCR and ILO supervisory mechanisms in Refugee law in which they construct supplementary institutions for non-party States, provide the applicability of refugee rights at national level.

Phase of Humanitarian Organizations' Bureaucratization

The controversial language of refugee and migration has been converted into humanitarian concern with the Displaced Persons Act strategy in 1948, which has been breakdown for refugees' identity as impoverished migrants. The second concern was the foundation of UNHCR in 1951 and its mission constitutive about refugee resettlement approach not only labour recruitment. The present frameworks of the refugees' and migrants' identities were constructed through political-humanitarian interests by international policy makers with no regard to economic contributions. Through ILO's migration administrative unanticipated practices engaged in migrants including refugees as workers since 1951, holding inter-governmental conference in Naples. In October 1951, Naples conference could have shown as a consequence of several conferences with multiplicity of action about migration policy by reason USA, Canada and Australia wholly rejected an organization with Soviet bloc states' members. Devising a collective action in this area the necessity to fulfill the relinquished auxiliary activities of IRO was thought as an urgent framework in world politics. Provisional Intergovernmental Committee for the Movement of Migrants from Europe (PICMME) has been supervisor after international conference *"Plan to Facilitate the Movement of Surplus Populations from Countries of Western Europe and Greece to Countries Affording Resettlement Overseas"* in Brussel, 26 November to 5 December 1951, represents democratic governments excluded Soviet bloc states.[15] PICMME had 16 member of states which constructed chiefly by USA to facilitate refugee and migrant regimes parallel to IRO's work, and later Intergovernmental Committee for European Migration (ICEM) entered into force 1954. ICEM had been tasked to arrange operations like from Southern Europe to Latin America and Australia. PICMME/ICEM' services haven't separate migration and refugee policy distinctly like ILO done.[16] In 1950's there was consensus between the correlation migrant policy and development issues, therefore International Organization for Migration (IOM) is a valve organization of UNHCR to convert into surplus manpower opportunity for the economic system rather than humanitarian principles. However, the international foundations of international refugee policy has been constructed on political base of anti-Soviet perspective curtailed refugees' freedom of movement around stringent measures, it had not yet been draw distinct line refugee and migrant identities by the way.

Expanding role of Intergovernmental Organizations in Global Refugee Governance

After Cold War, world politics challenge of binary world based on '*cultural*' differences and shift away from positivist theories to constructivist which could be characterized by multilateral communication.[17] The theoretical positioning of constructivist' like Alexander Wendt to provide explanations about IOs behavior' and the causes for the constitution of the outcomes, so the claim in this essay differs markedly in international relations approach. The essay suggests that IOs as autonomous actors and their propensity for inefficient outcomes, they produce in world politics. A combination of political science' normative and instrumental approaches have been used to reflect the interdisciplinary between international relations and international laws.[18] This could be assumed as a new lens towards constitution of international relations theories in the constructivist frame of ontology. Despite the attention of neoliberal institutionalists' treat to IOs as mechanism for state's exercising power, the international policies and tasks which they define, exemplification of their constitutive and purposive regime type. Related to essay's perspective regime literature is motivated by stations in semi-circle; individual ideas, social ideas, norms, mutual constitution and decision-making process like aspects of bureaucracies facilitate cooperation between states and IOs as Weber mentioned[19] Barnett and Finnemore view

[15] Long, op.cit., pp. 17-19.
[16] Reiko Karatani, "How History Separated Refugee and Migrant Regimes: In the Search of Their Institutional Origins", **International Journal of Refugee Law**, Vol. 17, No. 3, 2005, pp. 517-541.
[17] Antje Wiener, "Constuctivist Approaches in International Relations Theory: Puzzles and Promises", **Constitutionalism Webpapers**, Vol. 5, 2006, pp. 1-28.
[18] Robert O. Keohane, "International Relations and International Law: Two Optics", **Harvard International Law Journal**, Vol. 38, No. 2, 1997, pp. 487-502.
[19] Antje Wiener, "Constructivism: The Limit of Bridging Gaps", **Journal of International Relations**

IOs use authority to manage their mission and goals, and secondly IOs behaviors' *"shape bureaucrats perceptions of the world"*, and thirdly the consequences of their practices like tasks, categories, identities, models move beyond their founding purpose which is refer to *"bureaucratic pathologies"*.[20]

Emerging interrelations between UNHCR and ILO in the politics of international migration governance have a complex significant role reshaping state' with strategic exercise of power in refugee system. With characteristics like states both organizational hierarchies regulate bureaucratic culture the normative power could suffer from costs of expanded interstate cooperation and use opportunity as autonomous actors in world politics. Barnett and Finnemore accounts that IO authority derives from the ability to exercise power and illustrate the social world in this manner. In 1940s and 1950s were period of building international organizations have orientation to refugee and migration policies because of this reason their histories related to each other. While ILO' regulatory functions, normative instruments which were used to draw unique legitimacy on the right to work through conferences, conventions and recommendations. The pros and cons of ILO's tripartite structure enable to fulfill the deficits or gaps by procedural steps in the terms of policy and strategy developments. UNHCR' organization IOM governmentality associated with European Union institutions periphery. UNHCR and ILO share universal human right treaties: International Covenant on Economic, Social and Cultural Rights (ICESCR), International Covenant on Civil and Politic Rights, Convention on Elimination of all forms of Racial Discrimination, Convention on the Elimination of all forms of Discrimination against Women, the Convention on Rights of the Child including normative basis in the right to work.[21] The Refugee Convention on 1951 designed to ensure efficient recommendations to avoid discrimination over access job opportunities as nationals have. ILO' *"Convention No. 111 Convention concerning Discrimination in Respect of Employment and Occupation, 1958"*[22] uses norm-setting function to promote equal opportunity and treatment for employment to refugees and all workers. Legislative activities including migrant workers just as refugees provide to adopt measures for freedom of movement across the national borders.

The Mechanisms of Collaboration Between UNHCR and ILO in

---

and **Development**, Vol. 6, No. 3, 2003, pp. 252-275.

[20] Jacob Katz Cogan, "Review Work(s): Rules of the World: International Organizations in Global Politics by Michael Barnett and Martha Finnemore", **The American Journal of International Law**, Vol. 100, No. 1, 2006, pp. 278-281.

[21] Garnier, op.cit., p. 16.

[22] Convention No. 111 Convention concerning Discrimination in Respect of Employment and Occupation, ILO, Geneva, 1958, pp. 1-2.

Refugee Rights

ILO and UNHCR have technical collaborations have been appeared in 2003-2007 with "ILO-UNHCR Partnership through Technical Cooperation: Socio-economic Integration of Refugees, Returnees and Internally Displaced Persons" foundation. The exemplification of joint action addresses evolution from relief to Livelihoods Programmes for Refugees on July 2007 which received US$4,5 million in funding and intervened Mae Sot and Thailand. The Livelihoods Programmes (LHP) were intended to provide refugees income-generation opportunities and also integration of the host country' economic system by humanitarian assistance of implementing partners. By doing so refugees can contribute to local internal and external labour market, government policy requirements emphases on rising the standards of employment for the refugees like wage earning and income generation. The capacity of providing assistance mostly depends on generation of future income activities in provinces under consideration. Additional international organizations may also get involve to improve current situation in the terms of refugee livelihoods beneficent policy for both actors: refugee and the hosting country. Humanitarianism and impartiality bureaucratic culture creates a powerful controversy in the patterns of behavior articulated by international organizations. UN' pattern of behavior in order to set standards for the treatment of states towards immigration population sometimes come into conflict between moral patterns and humanitarian principles. In the core of sovereignty for national community perceived as well-managed borders to control entries in states' territories. IOM represent the double focus on international government of borders to conduct territorial regime both expectations of national policy and migration management, primarily plays crucial role in a borderless world after globalization.[23] IOM was well-known key institution engaged in cross- border policies in terms of humanitarian assistance for migration governance. The range of IOM' participation in border management interrelated within new regime regulations migrants and refugee policy. Rather than misleading contradictory sets of local environments' different historical experiences, international organizations assist voluntarily in norm-building to domestic government in the concern of hierarchical complexity which was induced by cultural contestation. It brings into focus that international regime complexity nature shape strategies for multiple power relation in world politics, and thereby political and social norm building legitimizing to each other under the state-induced return. However, the potential to confront the gaps for the consideration of refugee and migrant' for repatriation neither of home countries aim to constitute return-related policies.

---

[23] Kenichi Ohmae, The Next Global Stage Challenges and Opportunities in Our Borderless World, Pearson Education, New Jersey, 2007, pp. 18-20.

The promotion of essential components of UNHCR and ILO partnership to adopt the equal measures in labour market for refugees a regional, national and international level with signed Memorandum of Understanding (MoU) which were grounded with project in 1983.[24] UNHCR and ILO with regard to the protecting refugee' rights and integration at socio-economic areas transformation in refugee' right to gain a leading role in global politics. Generating an alternative perspective about IOs not only looking how are they exercising power like neoliberal institutionalism does, but also to emphasis on self-defeating consequences at the expense of their primary missions as constitutive bureaucracies. Further, this perspective can provide clarifications of how IOs rational legal power produce and conceptualize the social form in two facets impacts and consequences to international relations. In so doing, they enable us to investigate when international organizations are not beneficial servants of member' interest, why are they still normative or cultural powers in world politics. Although two broad strands; economistic and sociological theoretical approaches to organizations fit IOs in different ways by making certain assumptions, Weber's insight about IOs offers us the most complete e empirical conditions that we are analyzing about. Indeed, the strands of sociology describes social content of organizations rather than assuming organizations as arena or organization which have been defined according to other actors' interests. The sociologists' frameworks, especially Weber's, building on govern behavior in which to social control and power are embedded cultural and normative environment of bureaucracy. The power of IOs is embodied with legitimacy and knowledge[25] of technical expertise that two features have constitutive impacts with legal-rational authority. UNHCR and ILO construct a form of rational-legal authority in which creation of rules and actors due to their bureaucratic cultural missions. The virtues of new social form of bureaucracy exercise authority by performing duties and establishing norms makes IOs powerful. According to Weber, this bureaucratic control over other actors or willing to conduct set of normative values like recommendations, conferences and conventions carry out social purposes to legal space. Because of this reason Weber admires that evolvement in the IOs behavior may be desirable or not, but assumes this intend as *"good"*. On the other hand, international relations scholars criticize the Weber's insight IOs autonomic character in which is grounded on an independent authority rather than considered as mechanism for conducting new general rules. As it can be defined consequential but if we accept autonomous behavior of IOs like UNHCR authority has the expert status of refugee issues. The package of reforms established by UNHCR and ILO due to transforming international bureaucrats as their stated common

---

[24] Memorandum of Understanding between the International Labour Organization and the Office of the United Nations High Commissioner for Refugees, UNHCR and ILO, Geneva, 2016, pp. 1-5.
[25] IOs transform information into knowledge by analyzing information after orienting it to practice.

purpose will initiate beneficial or unintended conversion process. The discrepancies between practices and policies haven't been researched by international relations scholars since they have state-centric perspective. Barnett and Finnemore defines these consequences as bureaucratic pathologies as mentioned above, which can also interfere inter-agency cooperation.

From 1980s, the ILO, UNHCR and World Food Program (WFP) signed MoUs in treatments of refugee's right to work like socio-economic integration, developing job opportunities, exchanging policy. The following transformations of UNHCR focused on repatriation and ILO involved in labour supporting activities illustrate settings equality for refugees in accessing work. The cooperation of both IOs, *"ILO- UNHCR Partnership through Technical Cooperation: Socio Economic Integration of Refugees, Returnees and Internally Displaced Persons"*, which was supported by Italy has been established between 2003 and 2007.[26] The ILO-UNHCR Partnership through Technical Cooperation, Building Entrepreneurial Capacity for Returnee and Refugee Women in Angola and Mozambique on 2006 is an exemplification of collaboration that draw increasing attention to refugee livelihood rather than cooperating with financial issues. The UNHCR and ILO constitute a working group review projects to manage with other departments in the organizational framework. The implementation of UNHCR practical measures grounded in Global Compact of Refugees (GCR) which is representing key area for equal treatment of accessing to decent work, and also assists to local communities in their regulatory environments. The Global Refugee Forum is monitoring GCR, affirmed by UN General Assembly in 2019 to enhance opportunities of resettlement and decent work by coming together every four years.[27] Due to all of these contributions expanded arrangements improve working conditions, avoid from violation and discriminations of fundamental measures for refugees.

The Strengthening Protection Capacity (SPC) is good example of technical project between UNHCR-ILO in the context of enhancing refugees right to work, started with pilot implications in eight countries; Cameroon, Ecuador, Rwanda, Georgia, Thailand, The United Republic of Tanzania, Yemen and Zambia. From its foundation, 2005 to 2009 SPC Projects (SPCPs) have been expanded to a *"Global Initiative"* by executing Global Needs Assessment (GNA) in mentioned eight countries across the five continents. The SPCPs as an instrument of UNHCR-ILO collaboration figures out a map for the protection of refugees including budgets needed to improve livelihood gaps in protection capacity for refugees, built administrative capacity of the governments in host States. The SPCP

---

[26] Garnier, op.cit., pp. 15-25.
[27] See… **https://www.unhcr.org/global-refugee-forum.html** (Access: 24.09.2020).

activities mainstream the analyzing process protection gaps for the refugees and engaging a dialogue with States which are unwilling or in fragile situations and international organizations. The Department of International Protection Services legislative and administrative apparatus, The Department of Operational Services addressing registration and livelihoods issues, The Department of External Relations coordinate resources are operated technical baseline for the SPCPs as well as cooperating with ILO about self-reliance strategies. Indeed, SPCP creates publications in 2008: *"Protection Gaps: Framework for Assessing Gaps in Protection Capacity"*,[28] *"Protection of Conflict-Induced IDPs: Assessment for Action"*[29] can be seen as the inter-agency tool of refugee regime' construction.[30] The dissemination of the publications in the field was appearance of UNHCR recognized bilateral technical cooperation expanded on the normative level. Technical and financial assistance for the integration of refugees in order to maintain self-reliance have been promoted in regional and national contexts. In this regard, in 2006 UNHCR's Global Strategic Objectives (GSO) maintained to assist refugees current working situations which they are facing with globally. The ten objectives in which established to pursue cooperation with States in the creation of an international protection regime and other relevant actors. The publication UNHCR Global Appeal 2006 arrange to:

> "As part of the effort to institutionalize results-based management and mobilize action within the organization around a shared set of strategic objectives, the High Commissioner has established a series of measurable performance targets for 2006, articulated as quantifiable results, around a set of revised Strategic Objectives for 2006. The revised Strategic Objectives equally reprise the Agenda for Protection and contribute to the achievement of the Millennium Development Goals. These targets will be the focus of decision making and resource allocation in 2006".[31]

The framing of this paper provides instructive and fostering various problems in this instance articulation of humanitarian protection gaps on refugees right to work. Here international governmental organization interested with *"an institutional regime"* in order to determine the gaps and reconstruct frames of governance by targeting States to upgrade their immanent capacitating.[32] UNHCR's and ILO's facilitations are in similar vein

---

[28] Protection Gaps Framework for Analysis Enchanting Protection of Refugees Enhancing Protection of Refugees Strengthening Protection Capacity Project (SPCP), UNHCR, Geneva, 2008, pp. 1-86.

[29] Protection of Conflict-Induced IDPs: Assessment for Action, UNHCR, Geneva, 2008, pp. 1-96.

[30] See,https://www.unhcr.org/strengthening-protection-capacity.html#:~:text=The%20Strengthening %20Protection%20Capacity%20Project%20(SPCP)%20has%20been%20active%20in,the%20country% 2C%20and%20accelerating%20durable(Access: 26.09.2020).

[31] **Global Report 2005**, UNHCR, Geneva, 2006, p. 16.

[32] Rutvica Andrijasevic and William Walters, "The International Organization for Migration and the

the pilot implications, bilateral and multilateral projects among governments, which are complement each other in matters of refugees right to work. The promotion of capacity building process comes from in which States couldn't substitute the responsibility of international community' standards by projects of regional and national activities. Funding, technical expertise information and logistic support to disseminate the norms and standard might be demonstration of constitutive power of IOs. The creation of rules and actors are fertile ground for the new social form's spilling over into bureaucratic cultural missions about refugee protection policies. The involvements of UNHCR and ILO have complimentary structure within task sharing that goes beyond assessing gap in refugee policy literature. While international governmental organizations overarching normative frameworks for governments may support regional governments' measures rather than state-led implications to contribute state sovereignty in this manner.[33] The mentioned two autonomous actors' facilities embodied with their own missions, orientation and programs which practices as a bureaucracy. Nevertheless, the presence of bureaucracy' nature grounded on the accomplishment of their goals they play unanticipated roles for pathological behavior which have been conducted by the normative orientation of worldview. The absence of receiving "*feedback*" damages interrelated practices in their assessments, and it proceeds as follows: identifies bureaucratic cultural patterns among values from the environment whether it might applicable or not. Indeed, international governmental organizations do not evaluate their procedures on the account of their project's effectiveness. Secondly, their behavioral dispositions come from normative orientation of worldview construct a social form. Self-reliance projects like SPCPs not only sets out the legal institutional construction in refugee-hosting countries, but also maintaining decent jobs in the context of self-reliance policies which foster refugee-hosting States to make concessions to the demands of successful livelihood for refugees. Though, ILO has a leading role in integration of related measures, Thailand SPCPs project, UNHCR also design adequate policies and add values in livelihood as a partnership. The implementation of relevant laws and regulations for refugee right to work undermine self-reliance directly owing to the fact that UNHCR' autonomous policies shape refugee settlements among donors and asylum states view.[34] No matter how seriously UNHCR organized for protection of refugee rights, as IOs never engage in sustainable livelihoods. ILO publications within highlighting how the value of refugee skills-building; could be constituted in

International Government of Borders", **Environment and Planning D: Society and Space**, Vol. 28, No. 6, 2010, pp. 977-999.

[33] Anna Koch, "The Politics and Discourse of Migrant Return: The Role of UNHCR and ILO in the Governance Return", **Journal of Ethic and Migration Studies**, Vol. 40, No. 6, 2014, pp. 905-923.

[34] Meredith Hunter, "The Failure of Self Reliance in Refugee Settlements", **POLIS Journal**, Vol. 2, 2009, pp. 1-47.

policy field, besides this other international governmental organizations benefit from livelihood projects by integrating with UNHCR. On the contrary, ILO has not been conceptualized any added regulations in the field of refugee livelihoods governance as much as does UNHCR. Thirdly, likewise the two key actors in international refugee regime undermine refugee right to work by rationally established norms. According to neorealist and neo-liberals' literature because of focusing on material sources and information as power, they only concern about how IOs delineate the State behavior (bureaucratic culture) rather than norm-building feature of IOS in world politics.[35] While funds financial resources come from larger public bureaucracies, they are enable to mandate their policies to others within this kind of material power by IOs as autonomous actors. Thus, the degree and kind of IOs autonomy associated with State demands and interest, this created performance to satisfy political order maintains unexplained and unanticipated behavior we see. Both mechanisms' material resources and knowledge nourish bureaucracies in the same vein that have the characteristic of authority and autonomy by this way. The autonomy arises from authority, the implicit behavior in the specialized knowledge ensues the authority addition to its rational and impartial features. Weber also emphasis that the right to exercising authority generates the bureaucratic power and with bureaucratic powers it converts knowledge into general rules by building norms for the behavior of actors.

Conclusion

Seventy-six years ago, Roosevelt and Phelan have been signed The Declaration of Philadelphia, visionary document in order to construct global politics after the Second World War, which resonate with constitutional means of actions for ILO's powerful social mandate towards the promotion of the human rights for all people. The mismatch between the structure of the contemporary politics or realities and the style of discourse elaborated in ILO's constitution, have caused a deadlock politically because of the nature of the IOs. Reformulating deeply institutional practices of ILO have been framed in 2007 International Labour Conference (ILC), in order to establish efficacy for ILO's long-term practices by using 2008 Declaration on Social Justice for a Fair Globalization as a device. Legal richness of this device enunciates in the manner of both as an intergovernmental organization and its members even though it literally reconstructs the *"virtuous work"* within the ILO heretofore the prevention of unemployment according to the First International Labour Conference in 1919. The basic requirements containing in Article 41 *"Right to good administration"*[36] aims at conditions for weekly

---

[35] Barnett and Finnemore, op.cit.
[36] See… https://www.un.org/en/sections/un-charter/un-charter-full-text/ (Access: 24.08.2020).

working hours, adequate wages to maintain livelihoods in pre-war time contrary to unpredictable fragile situations[37] like civil conflict, financial crisis, pandemic (Covid19) which has been defined as *"positive social protection"* by Anthony Giddens. One of exemplification of the positive social protection is *"ILO's An Employers' Guide on Managing Your Workplace during COVID-19"*[38] establishes guidance about social security which ensures health regulations conducive to the role of refugees in the labour market integration. Working in partnership with UNHCR in order to overarching objectives; improvement in governance of the labour market, taking measures to avoid discrimination at work, enhancing legal status of refugees during employment and protecting refugee rights at global, regional and national levels with new regulations are priorities for the ILO. Power and expertise are core elements of refugee framework that must be addressed at international cooperation which fulfills an important role in the gaps of refugee protection regimes neither international law nor existing intergovernmental organizations have adequate global refugee governance architecture to manage alone. At the same time, the regional frameworks maintain a comprehensive approach to practical measures that concentrated at global level. In this sense ILO-UNHCR cooperation include the current problems in regional context as well as enhance strengthening mechanisms for protecting refugees right to work in order to accelerate their opportunities for livelihoods in host communities. The collaboration between these authorities work together to assist the fundamental rights of refugees through harmonized norm definition. As a part of the Syrian refugee crisis, the collaboration which has been signed on 1st July 2016, adopted to protect refugee' rights to work with integrated policies in the neighbouring countries affected as well as the hosting countries (International Labour Organization, 2016). On the other hand, knowledge (norm) diffusion between UNHCR-ILO can be regarded as bureaucratic universalism, cultural contestation and insulation within complexity of international environment. Barnett and Finnemore's research not only show the feature of the bureaucracies eclipse their goals which have been exhibited focus on expertise limits the vision of integration measures, and also explain how distinction between inter-agency collaborations defined by bureaucratic culture with actor's rationality. UNHCR focus mainly on recovery of livelihood and reintegration to their home country in the field which ILO acts as a knowledge provider. Although the UNHCR'S orientation on refugee workers can add values to consider the local context as much as universal standards resulting in ILO's normative realignment by their inter-agency cooperation. No matter how negative consequences arise

---

[37] Employment and Decent Work in Situations of Fragility, Conflict and Disaster, ILO, Geneva, 2016, pp. 1-172.
[38] An Employers' Guide on Managing Your Workplace During COVID-19, ILO, Geneva, 2020, pp. 1-34.

from that the larger international environment tailors the problem of regional and national governmentality activities to disseminate global governance policies.

CHAPTER 3

UNHCR'S DEMOGRAPHIC REPORTS ON REFUGEES

Ebru Gür* and Soyalp Tamçelik**

Introduction

The purpose of the current study is based on major contribution of population sciences including discipline of demography in the terms of refugee migration governance and policy, which utilizes steps for collecting data rather than assumption or myths in order to constitute management of refugees. The intersection between policy sciences and population sciences literature have a potential to outline future scenarios of populations and communities around the world including national, regional, social and environmental dynamics. There is an important role of analytic approach in enhancing capacity for demographic data collection concerning the refugee and forced migration, which enlightens policy development theoretically about adaptation and integration with operational and administrative processes. The foundations of international governmental organizations like UNHCR, Department of Economic and Social Affairs Population Division within the body of United Nations (UN), ILO, and International Organization for Migration (IOM) have essential frameworks for the policy relevant to refugee research.

Throughout this essay, the main focus indicated by its title demographic reports of UNHCR for Refugees, the essay's approach has been maintained that UNHCR's central functions in the terms of international refugee regime providing collection of accurate data including asylum seeker, refugees, internally displaced persons (IDPs) statistics. Improving common statistics have capacity, which serves an instrument to global politics about legislative regulations on refugee protection and mobilizing their resources with taken consideration into composition of the displaced communities moved away from home based upon environmental disasters, famine and conflict or violence. Thus, complexity of human trafficking which subjected to global issues recently should not be underestimated each element of political, financial, social and environmental sphere by disciplines primarily law,

* African Studies Ph.D. Student, Ankara Hacı Bayram Veli University, Department of International Relations, ORCID ID: 0000-0003-4791-3598, E-mail: ebrugur1@outlook.com.
** Prof. Dr.; Ankara Hacı Bayram Veli University, Faculty of Economics and Administrative Sciences, Head of International Relations Department, Turkey. E-mail: soyalp@hotmail.com. ORCID ID: 0000-0002-2092-8557

political science and international relations.

This essay demonstrates the benefit of using demographic research methodology to broaden the understanding of refugee problems' characteristics, the interrelationships between providing protection and developing policy, which concern about population mobility, dynamics of reintegration process to host or home countries. The engagement of demographic analysis' analytic perspective is valuable instrument to change multi-lateral efforts within the developing international refugee regime at national, regional and international levels. The first chapter will trace historical analysis of demographic data in the development of evidence-based programs building in both implementing protection and solutions for refugee problems. This will be introduced by transformation of geopolitical map within the context of political, social, and financial which also converts socio-economic area into more complex perspectives on refugee migrations for protection in twentieth century. Through theoretical approaches like neo-classical, transnationalism and social network focused on especially repatriation of refugees without any consideration to facts and dynamics of the results in various contexts.

The Office of the United Nations High Commissioner for Refugees (UNHCR) is a supervisor intergovernmental organization to support host governments according to 1951 United Nations Convention applying to the Status of Refugees with regulations, laws and administrative data systems including all effective parameters for international protection of refugees. The second chapter considers the study of demography of refugees associated with difficulties confronting the international refugee regime in which established practical steps and improvements by recruitment of professional statistician UNHCR on 1993. In the context of conventional refugee regime situations by the reason scholars have been working this issue as a quantitative data in exiting migration literature; we remarkably examine politics of refugee statistics to constitute a clear foundation for countries of origin, donor states, host states and humanitarian intergovernmental organizations with introducing illustrative case studies.

The Potential for Global Demographic Knowledge of Refugees

The critical role of demographic data which has been an important instrument developing policies, strategies at every level of governance to correlate refugee populations by monitoring the intersection between implementing Status of Refugees and considering social demographic data in registration, repatriation process. Different mechanisms on the stage of the crises like natural hazard, pandemic, political violence needs to be improved in host countries governance associate with factors of disasters for different forms temporary displacements throughout demographic and socio-economic variables of system by demographic analysis. The aggregate level of micro analysis identifying critical components to confront the social demographic composition at regional level and address implications of adaption and integration for the improvement of refugees' household welfare. The consequences of demographic research have subunit areas like enhancing comparative, longitudinal analysis beyond their assumptions or myths relating refugees. Models and future population scenarios have common technique among demographics that provides a wide range of possibilities about refugee' characteristics analytically rather than estimation of population. The exemplification for the concern to this potential of demography is International Institute for Applied Systems Analysis (IIASA), which illustrates research programs to serve alternative ways in order to constitute administrative, and operational systems with evidence- based information resources.[1]

The social constructivist' perspective on the account of international theory refugee law, international human rights and humanitarian law have interrelation between each other in some form of constructing normative structure.[2] Global governance could have exercised by actors like civil society neither a state nor an international governmental organization, which need to conform to international law in order to identify this, order *"constitutional"*. In a pluralist word system, this connection whichever angle it is interpreted, international law is not merely innocent about political influences re-designing regimes legitimately the professional role in charge of global governance. In the Universal Declaration of Human Rights stated that: *"Men and women of full age, without any limitation due to race, nationality or religion....* (Article16)"[3] the concept of nationality whom politicization of the refugee problems engaged in the protection of refugees. Indeed, 1951 United Nations Convention emphasizes the term 'refugee' neither having rights of the State nor a citizen of the country of origin, which is similar to that of stateless person. Many common challenges have come to embrace not only the field being nominally citizen but also discrimination in accessing to their fundamental rights by the reason having no international protection as a citizen of any another country. International community constitute a surrogate authority to UNHCR to fulfill refugee protection regime in the regard of United Nations instruments precisely normative and social level which serves States a framework for refugee issues. However, inflexibility on decision-making process goes beyond humanitarian international order in

---

[1] See, https://iiasa.ac.at/web/home/research/researchPrograms/AdvancedSystemsAnalysis/Overview. html (Access: 03.09.2020).

[2] Jan Klabbers and Touko Piriparinen, **Normative Pluralism and International Law,** USA, Cambridge University Press, 2013, p. 265.

[3] See, https://www.ohchr.org/EN/UDHR/Documents/UDHR_Translations/eng.pdf (Access: 03.09. 2020).

which the presence of power and politics by established universal categories legitimates unintended consequences by relating intergovernmental organizations. The dilemma about urgent situations, rules has no identifiable space with respect of basic human rights that confronts Genocide Convention in Rwanda as unique characteristics of given situation generally adapt different preexisting practices to maintain peace and security in 1994.[4]

The Issue of Refugee Statistics under Governmental Technology

The use of refugee management has been embodied with qualitative data somewhat difficult to tackle the holes of a crisis as a representation instrument for scattered community views both at global and local levels. The close resemblance between legal and bureaucratic norms should embody apolitical and impartial rules nevertheless, the transcendentalism develops cognitive shifts in the understanding of transformed practices of humanitarianism which may cause eliminating the root of the conflicts emerged. The humanitarian imperatives have been generated by most powerful States' pressure to decision making on codes of appropriate behavior exercising as a result of Weberian thought of traditional instrumental rationality. The production of harmonized refugee statistics has challenges and complex nature owing to the fact that variations on data sources and methods using to collect data for instance; population consensuses, surveys and administrative records may differ from country to country. *UN High Commissioner of Refugees and United Nations Relief and Works Agency for Palestine Refugees* (UNRWA) have contributed to ensure comparability of statistical units between countries for refugee populations by developing national standard definitions and adjustments. Besides, national and international system are interacting with each other which needs an important collaboration with both host countries, countries of origin in order to maintain standardized official statistics for policy making on national administrative levels as well as global governance structures. UNHCR' *Population Statistical Database* strengthening the nature of refugee statistics by synchronizing instruments of national and international coordination to achieve credibility, confidentiality, dissemination, independence on the world basis.

The conference that was held in Antalya, Turkey "*Report of the International Conference on Refugee Statistics*" recognizing the principles of being statistically significant for the production of official international statistics by Statistics Norway, Eurostat,[5] the Statistical Office of the European Free Trade

---

[4] See, https://www.un.org/en/preventgenocide/rwanda/preventing-genocide.shtml (Access: 20.08. 2020).

[5] See, https://ec.europa.eu/eurostat/data/database (Access: 18.08.2020).

Association (EFTA), Turkish Statistical Institute (TurkStat) and UNHCR.[6] The international organizations and national statistical experts especially have discussed about the usage of administrative data, registration for refugee protection, the existing methods on how the information collecting demographic data through subsystems in every country in this conference.

Pathways for Demographic Aggregated Data within the Scope of Refugee Complex Temporalities

The presence of country variations as identifiers considered and application of legal instruments for refugee population has not served a uniform system, so *United Nations Economic Commission for Europe* (UNECE) is a World Forum for Harmonization of Vehicle Regulations (WP.29) within including three UN agreements in 1958, 1997 and 1998 (Global Technical Regulations/ UN GTRs) develops a legal framework for member countries. First of all, in this study the term *"refugee and refugee related populations"* have preferred to use throughout UNHCR documents referring to refugees, asylum seekers, returned refugees, groups in refugee-like situations except stateless persons and internally displaced persons (IDPs) in the scope of statistical measurement. Although IDPs have recommendations in the IDP Technical Report, unfortunately stateless persons are excluded from this kind of international protection by the reason of not facing the same level persecution like refugees.[7] Multiple approaches have been used for source of refugee demographic statistics, the distinctive discrepancies between Norwegian and United Kingdom (UK) statistics derives from adopting UNHCR regulations on a regional level. For example, a person entered to the Norway considered as a refugee in statics; however, refugee statistics depends on evaluation of asylum applications which given residence status may change across time.[8] The procedure of UNHCR mandate refugee status determination conducted as a statutory responsibility as provided in 1951 Convention by applying three main steps only for asylum-seekers from Europe. The first procedure application for refugee status and then application has been reviewed by authorities and afterwards the claim of refugees status adjudicated by the system.

UNECE proposed initiative to enhance the common definitions for the methodology of national statistical officials with *Principles and Recommendations for the 2020 Censuses of Population and Housing,* by this way high quality data will

---

[6] Report of the International Conference on Refugee Statistics, UNHCR, Antalya, 2015, pp. 1-20.
[7] Bela Hovy, "Registration-A Sine Qua Non for Refugee Protection", **Demography of Refugee and Forced Migration**, Graeme Hugo, Mohammad Jalal Abbasi-Shavazi, Ellen Perey Kraly (Ed.), Switzerland, Springer International Publishing, 2018, p. 41.
[8] Expert Group on Refugee and Internally Displaced Persons Statistics International Recommendations on Refugee Statistics, EUROSTAT, Luxemburg, 2017, p. 136.

provide to deal with global ongoing refugee crisis.[9] UNECE stated recommendations in order to come to a common understanding about usual resident population *"…The place at which the person has lived continuously for at least the last 12 months, not including temporary absences for holidays or work assignments, or intends to live for at least 12 months"* in this approach also accepted by experts and officials in the Conference of European Statisticians Recommendations for the 2020.[10] It is not only important to establish systems for collection of data but also administrative principles can be adopted in the regardless of common criteria. The high quality of statistics has fundamental role in political and administrative support by ensuring about enumeration instructions that provides long-term planning and service delivery effectively at sub-national levels. *The Department of Economic and Social Affairs* lead to improve economic, social and environmental data which is vital for translating policy frameworks among instutional and organizational arrangements as a department of UN Secretariat. The implementation of international refugee regime has been a fundamental responsibility interlinking within demographic and geographic variables compiled from administrative data of countries in intergovernmental bodies to advice policy and strategy option for refugees and related populations. The production of standardisation of statistical data collection techniques, coordination mechanisms at national, regional and international levels to enable to make clear legal basis of system for refugee status.

The concept of repatriation or return to homeland has unique dynamics and challenges which will lead to focus on demographic, social and economic analysis as well as managing the difficulties in registration process. Demographic characteristics of refugees as mentioned earlier has been integrated to social and institutional circumstances at host countries, so that mostly the global demographic statistics monitoring where UNHCR data collection programmes are aggregated at local level. Reflecting on the meaning of permanent solutions for the problem of international protection by governments or intergovernmental organizations during the transformation of geo-political map have been outlined voluntary repatriation, alternative resettlement schemes reintegration into home society. After the nature of boundaries had been changed globally, migration and migration typologies return to multifaced phenomenon which population mobility classified as *"voluntarily or involuntarily/forced movement"* by Peterson. According to Peterson' analysis designated four units of measurements migrants have decisive changing their level of aspirations with taking important consideration to environmental factors from voluntary

[9] **Principles and Recommendations for the 2020 Censuses of Population and Housing Censuses,** UN Department of Economic and Social Affairs Statistics Division, New York, 2017, pp. 1-136.
[10] Conference of European Statisticians Recommendations for the 2020 Censuses of Population and Housing, UNECE, Geneva, 2015, pp. 1-251.

movement to forced movement.[11] There has been growing efforts to differentiate using as semantics '*refugee migration*' to identify forced migration or involuntary migration in some cases after analysis have been conducted to '*systems*' beyond the '*individual level*' in literature.

The 1951 Convention centrepiece of international refugee regime has been considered post-Second World War circumstances in which these limitations removed with the 1967 United Nations Protocol on Refugees besides progressive development of international human rights law.[12] The protection of persons whom persecuted owing to political view, nationality, race, has been endorsed in 1951 Convention afterwards non-discrimination on the grounds of sex, age, disability and other prohibited area, the universal coverage of non-refoulement applied as a safeguard against threats about lives or freedom of refugees in any manner with 1967 Protocol. As a result of expanding definition of refugee, both UNHCR and UNWRA applying refugee status to all persons under pressure of an external force like political pressure and conflicts thanks to 1967 Protocol obliges to States with unlimited accession as an independent instrument.[13] Even though UNHCR has been seen as exempfilication of the apolitical and humanatarian international bureaucracy, the operational role and also assited to the host country about refugee repatriation could involved in political sphere. As a result of expanded mission of UNHCR from legal protection of refugees to assisting for "*nonstatutory refugees*" with new mechanisms like offices, this depoliticization in the framework of humanatarian issues promote organizational activities throughout the world. The distinction between the various perpectives about repatriation especially appeared this issue mentioned as a solution for refugee and migration problems during two World Wars, anti-colonial movements, and also in 1990s was called '*repatriation period*', whereas after the Cold War the pace of refugee population change has accelarated and they simultaneously become new actors of civil wars. The theoretical insights how repatriation has been analyzed by neoclassical economics, the new economics of labour migration, structuralism, transnationalism and social network theory considering different sets of criteria so as to dealt with the dynamic of repatriation.

The main challenges for the meaning of '*return to home*' and '*repatriation*' comes from repatriation refers to a status in which have been assisted by UNHCR or governments, but this term has been generally used interchangeably with the term return. The politicisation of refugee regime policies adopted by UNHCR and governmental bodies shifted from

---

[11] William Peterson, " Ageneral Typology of Migration", **American Sociological Review**, Vol. 23, No. 3, pp. 256-266.

[12] Convention and Protocol Relating to the Status of Refugees, UNHCR, Geneva, 2010, pp. 1-56.

[13] Migration, Development and Environment, IOM, Geneva, 2008, pp. 1-68.

sovereignity to human rights between 1970s to 1980s, the end of Cold War internal wars were growing in illiberal systems notably threatening international community on the grounds of peace and security. Hence, the structural turn in the discourse of international governance globally was becoming tolerant the involvement in domestic policies with the opportunity given to international organizations, specifically UNHCR on the account of repatriation. Returning to home become one of the most critical issue in world politics currently due to widespread conflicts and wars that was not a suprise, both communities and goverments neighbouring emphasize refugee and forced migration as a problem. Narratives carrying solutions for contentment about various solutions of refugee flows were accompanied by social demographic data which is critical issue for refugees in the terms of return, repatriation and reintegration processes.

Human security was strengthened in UNHCR agendas since the complexness of refugee and forced migration was prevalent with increasing momentum through international collaborations, as taking measures in XXI. Century. *Millenium Development Goals for 2015* establishing principles for the close interest to protect the human rights of international and refugee migration which decided to resolve in Resolution 55/2 adopted by UN General Assembly in September 2000.[14] UN High-Level Summit for Refugees and Migration has been a well laid plan in the UN Report of Secretary General named *"In Safety and Dignity: Addressing Large Movements of Refugees and Migrants"* in which the demand for data collection should considerably easier while, at the same time international dialogue and practices helped them preserve refugee and refugee related populations from unintended consequences of global or regional turmoils.

It is remarkable to renew the understanding of resemblance between international and domestic order including the security dialogue among characteristics of States rather than sovereignty by focusing demographic lens to the drivers of international migration. Whereas some of analytical framewoks differ in their analyse levels with respect to theories presented about return to origin countries whatever the theoretical insights reflecting emprical approaches or official quantitive data, understanding the set of variables in the field of migration aims to illustrate the circumstances of multi-polar mobility of migrants.[15] Despite comparative analysis of these theories the contribution on the development of return migraton literature they are playing significant role in bearing about return phenomenon

---

[14] Ellen Percy Kraly and Mohammad Jalal Abbasi-Shavazi, "The Promise and the Potential of the Demography of Refugee and Forced Migration", **Mobilizing Global Knowledge: Refugee Researchin an Age of Displacement**, Susan McGrath and Julie E.E. Young (Ed.), University of Clagary Press, 2019, p. 171.

[15] Jean Pierre Cassarino, "Theorising Return Migration: The Conceptual Approach to Return Migrants Revisited", **International Journal on Multicultural Studies**, Vol. 6, No. 2, 2004, pp. 264-276.

linkages between politicization of international refugee regime and intergovernmental organizations.

The Reception of Demographic Methodology by UNHCR

The policies adopted by UNHCR actively built upon ensuring repatriation of refugees on the need to promote human rights and economic development in domestic space that reconstructed among '*state responsibility*'. In fact, the vision of UNHCR being involved in new functions after 1980s refugees not only beneficiary of this both humanitarian and political process but also UNHCR embodied with good offices, which allows demonstrating protection and assistance in an apolitical manner. These two related controversial issues emerged under humanitarianism and apolitical manner by using refugee law and the principle of sovereignty challenge for UNHCR's role generating repatriation and reintegration concepts in world politics.[16] The refugee regime policies adopted by UNHCR, after 1980s, the refugee regime policies were impacted by important transformation, in the meaning of the way to maintain international peace and security concern to monitoring politics between the borders rather than politics within borders. The shift in understanding of '*normative and legal environment*' UNHCR mechanisms take preventive action in order to eliminate the risks for refugees inherently embrace the reconstruction of local structure; the bureaucratization might go beyond apolitical humanitarism to politicization under the basic principles of funding States for governance structure.[17] UNHCR has documented the demographic data for the population in which maximizes the protection for refuge and related populations with policies developed for recurrent problems through integrated administrative data. Moreover, this evidence-based system enable to forecasting refuge and related populations in the concept of humanitarian crises at global and regional levels. The New York Declaration for Refuges and Migrants, meeting on 19th September 2016, one of the platforms that paved the way for both *Global Compact on Refugees* and *Global Compact for Safe, Orderly and Regular Migration* that political declaration represents unprecedented effect on the purpose of fulfilling the gap between international refugee regime and "state responsibility".[18] The affirmation of the "*Comprehensive Refugee Response Framework (CRRF)*" in this declaration makes a significant contribution to global solidarity with wide ranging key

---

[16] Soyalp Tamçelik ve Talip Menekşe, "Uluslararası Sistemde Başarılı Göç Yönetim Modelleri Kapsamında Türk İltica Sistemi'ne Özgü Yeni Bir Göç Yönetim Modeli Denemesi: Karar Merkezleri", **II. Uluslararası Göç ve Mülteci Kongresi Bildirileri**, Prof. Dr. İlhan GENÇ ERTAN, Doç. Dr. Metin KILIÇ, Dr. Öğr. Ü. Şevket Ercan KIZILAY, Dr. Öğr. Cihan Ü., Düzce, Düzce Üniversitesi Yayınları, 2019, pp. 585-615.

[17] Michael N. Barnett, Security and Governance Series: The International Humanatarian Order, London, Routledge, 2010, p. 10.

[18] See, https://www.unhcr.org/new-york-declaration-for-refugees-and-migrants.html (Access: 18.09.2020).

objectives for refugee protection on the grounds of registration, repatriation and reintegration policies as stated in its objectives part "*....(i) ease pressures on host countries; (ii) enhance refugee self-reliance; (iii) expand access to third country solutions; and (iv) support conditions in countries of origin for return in safety and dignity...*".[19] With the *Global Compact for Safe, Orderly and Regular Migration* is a milestone for developing statistical measures throughout the nations with twenty-three objectives harmonizes solutions for massive displacements in international humanitarian landscape. Data about demographic composition is also important as mentioned within objectives which cooperative framework built upon this draft, the first objective is "*Collect and utilize accurate and disaggregated data as a basis for evidence-based policies*" indeed dispersing clear information about benefits and challenges for refugee and refugee related populations across the world.[20] A decade long analysis of demographic data has become indispensable for distribution of resources in urgent situations and monitoring the future size of population, since the Demographic Projection Tool (DPTool) design to access updated information, which can provide statistical and comprehensive data for a standard guidance of decision making in operational, political concepts.

The size of rising figures refugees, asylum-seekers, IDPs (forcibly displaced) indeed stateless persons and related groups have been accompanied with protecting UNHCR despite the fact that they are not entitle to.[21] This kind of valid data generated statistically by UNHCR may respond not only needs for the world's forcibly displaced persons' but also growing attention to finding solutions about displacement. With the insights of some writers expanded the definitions of forces recognized by UNHCR in order to assist displaced persons in which including natural disasters such as related to climate change in their countries of origin. Thus, El-Hinawi found a new way to identify "environmental refugee" that has been focused on supporting human life mechanisms as well as displacement, in this created spectrum UNHCR and IOM defined another classification '*Environmentally Displaced Persons* (EDPs)' within different international regime from IDPs.[22]

The literature on refugees and refugee related populations within in the framework of international law and policy transformed by a call for more advanced data to use an objective guidance for the reflecting the unique characteristics of each population movements. The availability of access to statistical data obtaining from governments and intergovernmental organizations have been updated on a harmonized platform called as "*ProGres*

---

[19] **Global Compact on Refugees**, UN, New York, 2018, pp. 1-60.

[20] Tamçelik and Menekşe, op.cit., pp. 585-615.

[21] The UNHCR Demographic Projection Tool: Estimating the Future Size and Composition of Forcibly Displaced Populations, UNHCR, Geneva, 2018, pp. 1-22.

[22] **Environmental Refugees**, UNEP, Nairobi, 1985, p. 41.

v.4" during the registration and follow-up activities neither deny access on input or sharing data to public domain but also disaggregated data available online for them. The deployment of using these data in relevant situations depends on adequacy in registration process including individual-level data like gender, age, country of origin, date of birth, date of arrival or registration as UNHCR collected micro data in registration affects analysis from preliminary level in the manner of population projections. UNHCR prefers to use cohort-component method in projection of population, after Bayesian hierarchical models illustrating the long-term model to enhance the scenarios about fertility, mortality and according to these "Medium" projections for the international migration rates represented with '*Low*' or '*High*' values by UNHCR.[23] At the heart of cohort-component method lies the predetermined possibilities with any concern to aggregated data in spite of the fact that scientists express the error of future possibilities may not cover the world distribution. Bayesian hierarchical models, added 12 or more data that provide stabilization of the estimations by leading five more parameters for different countries at every level of fertility rate and life expectancy for males and females with variations in long-term.[24] For probabilistic projections of UNHCR the interrelation between countries must be taken into account by the reason of deterministic projections is also included regions and unity of countries on economic, political and environmental area and this figures out the essential role of future works due to overcome kinds of refugee statistical challenges after all.

The demographic populations must meet three certain changing criteria as considered by UNHCR; "*natural increase, forced displacement, resettlement, changes in administrative structure*" determined among 130 countries where including different the types operational area in management of UNHCR's system (UN High Commissioner for Refugees, 2018). Persons of concern (PoC) is a key indicator of DPTool that has been developed by Field Information and Coordination Support Section (FICSS) in 2017-2018 so as to conduct '*demographic projection methodologies*' introducing age, sex, origin and type of population with ProGress v.4 system for every three year in UNHCR operations. DPTool configured out by DemProj Model in Spectrum to combine assumption about demographic pattern in the context of cohort component model and one-year launched statistical data of population composed of inputs; sex and age, fertility and life expectancy rates and also forced migration.[25] The right to be registered at birth, deaths and

[23] The UNHCR Demographic Projection Tool: Estimating the Future Size and Composition of Forcibly Displaced Populations, UNHCR, Geneva, 2018, pp. 1-22.
[24] Adrian E. Raftery and Patrick Gerland, Leontine Alkema, "Bayesian Population Projections for the United Nations", **Statistical Science**, Vol. 29, No. 1, 2014, pp. 58-68.
[25] John Stover and Sharon Kirmeyer, **DemProj Version 4 Manual: A Computer Program for Making Population Projections**, Futures Group International, 2007, pp. 1-106.

underreporting registrations play a key role in enumeration of demographic populations, so could impact estimations about fertility and mortality in other words the these given inputs have been intertwined with cohort component projections. Innovation Service has been constructed a platform to provide data about population flows (arrivals and departures) within UNHCR to reach reliable demographic data by planting Jetson application since 2018.

The innovation facility moving forward to measure misaligned indicators owing to *'long-term transformative goals'* practices; that's why co-designing processes was embodied with technology in entrepreneurial offices where exploring tools to bringing the dynamics of population flows to the table.[26] At the heart of defining solutions and addressing gap between humanitarian need and resource management was robust demographic methods and, as a result UNHCR enables to improve national and global estimates for policy-making, programming and distribution of resources. As mentioned before the DPTool initially obtaining demographic rates from World Population (WPP) afterwards uses assumptions like *"the country of asylum refers to life expectancy at birth"* and then with data about displacements (arrivals and departure) they figure out mortality and forced migration, the last stage also including estimation in the age and sex contexts. With this reporting process, the available data in progress v.4 resemble the age and sex composition of the last year, UNHCR country offices need to improve the primary data processing which collection method annotated with various methods and sources with surveys, censuses at registration and repatriation levels.

The demographic composition of refugee populations is one of the major issues confronting the international refugee regime in which categories and definitions established for the global community' future; however, meeting challenges among the implications of evidence-based policies for the demography needs protection. A case study of South Sudanese refugees in Kenya should illustrate opportunities for policy related to demographic composition of refugees as well as challenges dealing with socially, economically and demographically. The demographic composition of refugee populations has been associated with older populations who are not able to avoid from forced recruitment on because of physical disabilities while highlighting the displacement internally and to host countries like Uganda for South Sudan.

UNHCR's country level data on segments of displaced population must take consideration into the non-displaced populations and the availability of disaggregated data from countries of origin as a result the estimation techniques depending on methodological choices targeted into these

[26] See, https://www.unhcr.org/innovation/innovation-metrics-for-human-development-what-have-we-learned/ (Access: 22.09.2020).

processes. Exploring the international mobility of populations, it is necessary to explaining in demographic lens during the crisis timeframe specification of displacement flows, DPTool used for the projection of alternative scenarios. Ideally, the size of the future refugee flows should have a standardized method for, whereas the launch population of South Sudanese refugees in Kenya derived from the last year' ProGres data within UNHCR. Because of the fact that assumptions about population flow aimed at promoting a comprehensive source of statistical information in which other parameters have been taken as standing data, whereby previous arrivals and experience of officers pave the way for low, medium and high periods. The estimates modified with the *"fertility rates of the country of origin"* and *"mortality rates of the country of destination"* by taking previous years' age and sex as variables into account in DPTool and finally the tool has been figured out three different assumptions for the mentioned three scenarios till to end of year populations. Not only DPTool data have the ability to protect refugee and refugee related populations, but also producing standardized outputs with an error as a result of unforeseeable sharp changes during the prolonged armed conflict in Sudan. Hence, the problems with the quality of demographic data collected and insights that have been conducted by UNHCR's professionals should differ somewhat from reality owing to fact that assumption of demographic change affects the DPTool actually. In some instances, the quality of ProGres data may be superior in illustrating how traditional demographic methods could be applied for the future development with cohort component projections in order to fulfill the goal about demographic disaggregation. Furthermore, the ProGres v.4 data system is available since 2015, which helps to promote the methodological gap in registration level updating older versions despite changes in political and social landscapes.

The combined impact of reproduction in digital infrastructures involving power asymmetries and exclusions about unifying variables which have a direct result of politic order standing within UNHCR funding States. The political authority of States speaks their own truths while at the same time pursuing objectives big distinct from UNHCR' refugee regime. In the line with this approach the main emphasis will be in the history of humanitarianism measured by the intergovernmental organizations, in January 2018, 1.4 million mass influx of refugees reported in Uganda because of the violence in South Sudan which is under- informed by UNHCR and Uganda's Office of the Prime Minister (OPM). Even though one of the largest refugee settlement in the world was in Uganda with its designated areas in hillsides, in which refugee settlements have been constructed upon OPM's 'open-door refugee policy', the realization of this event reveal that decision making procedures within both UNHCR and OPM were not sure how to manage health, education and security problems for the increasing population flow. In these refugee settlements near borders are unique since they are not structures like camps, refugees have opportunity to farm on a 50 meters plot square and in addition to this, and they could trade with the communities in Uganda according to OPM's historical agreements. BidiBidi[27] hosted officially registered 1,2 million refuge represent a snapshot of the timeline that suggested with a realistic estimate approach, the territorial intersection between Uganda and South Sudan identifies designated locations to authorities despite unknowns about demographic variables of current influxes.

Conclusion

The accumulation of refugee complexities holistically generated from the differences in UNHCR and government registration processes about statistical reports, policies and also challenge of human factors, so as to operate coordination issues Comprehensive Refugee Response Coordination (CRRF) has been established within UNHCR.[28] Hard as UNHCR work with official and intergovernmental organizations in the capable of accommodation of local priorities for the success of refugee management, geographical scale of Uganda could not result in resource allocation efficiency with lack of engagement about the set of statistics on unknowns within refugee settlements. Though the technological solutions about digital data collection sustain helpful handover to local and national governance, the authorities in Uganda worrying the implications whether new humanitarian mechanisms create situations fit for purpose or not. The disinclination to engage with value from innovations in Africa originated from colonial period, whereas introduction of new technologies have been increasingly inevitable across the world when dealing with humanitarian action. As many efforts to tackle on the refugee management issue focused by UNHCR, general challenge among 'implementing partners' on application of mechanisms at local level could never prevent the holes in demographic data. In short, the up-to-date information on refugee needs highly efficient to contribute with the combination of qualitative and quantitative data approaches by working together on the grounds of every community' social, geographical, political pictures. As a result of recognition global mobility in which borders have gradually diminished associated with globalization somewhat cooperative or adaptive to international refugee regime in this emerging global momentum. It is clear that "*multi-causality of population movement*" has need for infrastructural system through the support from intergovernmental organizations like

---

[27] The map which shows BidiBidi settlement with all resources in Yumbe District. https://umap.openstreetmap.fr/it/map/bidibidi-refugee-settlement-base-mapping_245242#11/3.4480/31.3770 (Access: 22.08.2020).

[28] Rupert Alan, "Modalities of United Statelessness", **Mapping Crisis Participation, Datafication and Humanitarism in the Age of Digital Mapping**, Specht Doug (Ed.), London, University of London Press, 2020, pp. 217-252.

UNHCR in a community self-governance sociopolitical environment.[29] The ways in terms of increasing pace of refugee and refugee related populations have divergent views from different member States neither negative nor positive, but evidence data-based plays necessary and critical role during the construction of the demographic data for neutrality both in political agendas and governmental practices as a reflection on the subjectivity of statistical data. Thus, the consideration given to the complex temporalities of qualitative data collection world in the context of protection for refugee and refugee related populations should be encountered into while emerging in a borderless world.

---

[29] Giovanna Astolfo, Ricardo Marten Caceres, Garyfalia Palaiologou, Camillo Boano and Ed Manley, "The Role of Data Collection, Mapping and Analysis in the Reproduction of Refugeness and Migration Discourses: Reflections from Refugee Spacesproject", **Mapping Crisis Participation, Datafication and Humanitarism in the Age of Digital Mapping**, Specht Doug (Ed.), London, University of London Press, 2020, pp. 120-142.

CHAPTER 4

THE SUSTAINABLE DEVELOPMENT GOALS (SDGS) AND MIGRANTS / MIGRATION

İsmail Melih Baş[*]

Introduction

The Global Risks Report which is prepared and issued every year by the World Economic Forum (WEF) is known widely all over the globe. Taking a look at the Reports from 2007 on 2020 will show us that "**involuntary migration**" is one of the "Top 5 Global Risks in Terms Likelihood" as well as "Top 5 Global Risks in Terms of Impact".[1] The impacts are considered in different areas which are intercorrelated strictly. These areas (economic – environmental- societal) are named as "triple bottom line"[2] and reported with an integrated style like "integrated reporting"[3] or "GRI reporting".[4]

Sustainable develeopment as a buzzword through the last few decades is seen as a panacea (something that will solve all problems or cure all illnesses). Is it so really? Some says it is a lullaby![5] Some says instead of this concept, the term "sustainable living" could be preferred. Also this term is popular globally.[6]

Another super interesting way of thinking about sustainable living is using the concept of Doughnut Economics, developed by visionary thinker and Economist, Kate Raworth. This concept uses big picture thinking to help redefine how our global and local systems can operate such that we live within our means as humanity (i.e., sustainably).

---

[*] Prof. Dr. İstanbul Arel Üniversitesi, İİBF. melihbas@arel.edu.tr@arel.edu.tr, ORCID ID: 0000-0003-1455-9529
[1] WEF, The Global Risks Report 2020, Switzerland, WEF Publications, 2020
[2] John Elkington, "25 Years Ago I Coined the Phrase "Triple Bottom Line." Here's Why It's Time to Rethink It", Harvard Business Review, 25.6.2018. https://www.forbes.com/sites/jeroenkraaijenbrink/2019/12/10/what-the-3ps-of-the-triple-bottom-line-really-mean/?sh=2ea38c3c5143 (Access 3.1.2021)
[3] IIRC, "Integrated Reporting Framework 2020 Revision", https://integratedreporting.org/, (Access 3.1.2021)
[4] GRI, "How to use the GRI standards", https://www.globalreporting.org/how-to-use-the-gri-standards/get-started-with-reporting/ (Access 3.1.2021)
[5] Thomas Pogge and Alnoor Ladha, " The Sustainable Development Goals: A Siren And Lullaby For Our Times", https://www.occupy.com/article/sustainable-development-goals-siren-and-lullaby-our-times#sthash.1mQ3iJsn.dpbs, (Access 3.1.2021)
[6] Sustainablejungle, "What is sustainable living", https://www.sustainablejungle.com/sustainable-living/what-is-sustainable-living/, (Access 3.1.2021)

As she puts it on her website:

"Humanity's 21st century challenge is to meet the needs of all within the means of the planet. In other words, to ensure that no one falls short on life's essentials (from food and housing to healthcare and political voice), while ensuring that collectively we do not overshoot our pressure on Earth's life-supporting systems, on which we fundamentally depend – such as a stable climate, fertile soils, and a protective ozone layer.
The Doughnut of social and planetary boundaries is a playfully serious approach to framing that challenge, and it acts as a compass for human progress this century.".[7]

However, is Sustainable Development **worth the trouble?** People and organizations that are in favor of sustainable development believe that it's worth moving past these disadvantages to work on the environment. Advocates say that sustainable development is an investment in future generations. The biggest defenders of these initiatives are working on ways of overcoming the hurdles.

In order to make Sustainable Development concept work, an agenda for a framework is designed: 2030 Agenda which includes 17 Sustainable Development Goals (SDGs). For each goal some targets (totally 169) are determined; and also for each target some indicators (totally 232) designed as well.

Brief history of SDGs

"The 2030 Agenda for Sustainable Development, adopted by all United Nations Member States in 2015, provides a shared blueprint for peace and prosperity for people and the planet, now and into the future. At its heart are the 17 Sustainable Development Goals (SDGs), which are an urgent call for action by all countries - developed and developing - in a global partnership. They recognize that ending poverty and other deprivations must go hand-in-hand with strategies that improve health and education, reduce inequality, and spur economic growth – all while tackling climate change and working to preserve our oceans and forests. Transforming our world: the 2030 Agenda for Sustainable Development with its 17 SDGs was adopted at the UN Sustainable Development Summit in New York in September 2015. Now, the annual High-level Political Forum on Sustainable Development serves as the central UN platform for the follow-up and review of the SDGs. Today, the Division for Sustainable

---

[7] Kate Raworth, "What on Earth is the Doughnut?", https://www.kateraworth.com/doughnut/# (Access 3.1.2021)

Development Goals (DSDG) in the United Nations Department of Economic and Social Affairs (UNDESA) provides substantive support and capacity-building for the SDGs and their related thematic issues including water, energy, cilmate, oceans, urbanization, transport, science and technology, the Global Sustainable Development Report (GSDR), partnerships and Small Island Developing States. DSDG plays a key role in the evaluation of UN systemwide implementation of the 2030 Agenda and on advocacy and outreach activities relating to the SDGs. In order to make the 2030 Agenda a reality, broad ownership of the SDGs must translate into a strong commitment by all stakeholders to implement the global goals. DSDG aims to help facilitate this engagement".[8]

A Bird's Eye View of SDGs

The SDGs may be acronymed as 5Ps as a pentagon (Don't confuse it with Pentagon – the headquarters building of US Department of Defence, please). These letters are explained by UN as follows:

People : We are determined to end poverty and hunger, in all their forms and dimensions, and to ensure that all human beings can fulfil their potential in dignity and equality and in a healthy environment.

Planet: We are determined to protect the planet from degradation, including through sustainable consumption and production, sustainably managing its natural resources and taking urgent action on climate change, so that it can support the needs of the present and future generations.

Prosperity : We are determined to ensure that all human beings can enjoy prosperous and fulfilling lives and that economic, social and technological progress occurs in harmony with nature.

Peace : We are determined to foster peaceful, just and inclusive societies which are free from fear and violence. There can be no sustainable development without peace and no peace without sustainable development.

Partnership: We are determined to mobilize the means required to implement this Agenda through a revitalised Global Partnership for Sustainable Development, based on a spirit of strengthened global solidarity, focussed in particular on the needs of the poorest and most vulnerable and with the participation of all countries, all stakeholders and all people.

The interlinkages and integrated nature of the Sustainable Development

---

[8] UN Department of Economic and Social Affairs, "Goals", https://sdgs.un.org/goals, (Access 3.1.2021)

Goals are of crucial importance in ensuring that the purpose of the new Agenda is realised. If we realize our ambitions across the full extent of the Agenda, the lives of all will be profoundly improved and our world will be transformed for the better".[9]

Because of the main topic of this book is "migration", i could go beyond the limit, if i allocate pages for explanation of the SDGs. However, for the readers it will be fruitful to list short definitions for SDGs (Table 1).

Table 1 : Sustainable Development Goals

Goal 1. End poverty in all its forms everywhere
Goal 2. End hunger, achieve food security and improved nutrition and promote sustainable agriculture
Goal 3. Ensure healthy lives and promote well-being for all at all ages
Goal 4. Ensure inclusive and equitable quality education and promote lifelong learning opportunities for all
Goal 5. Achieve gender equality and empower all women and girls
Goal 6. Ensure availability and sustainable management of water and sanitation for all
Goal 7. Ensure access to affordable, reliable, sustainable and modern energy for all
Goal 8. Promote sustained, inclusive and sustainable economic growth, full and productive employment and decent work for all
Goal 9. Build resilient infrastructure, promote inclusive and sustainable industrialization and foster innovation
Goal 10. Reduce inequality within and among countries
Goal 11. Make cities and human settlements inclusive, safe, resilient and sustainable
Goal 12. Ensure sustainable consumption and production patterns
Goal 13. Take urgent action to combat climate change and its impacts*
Goal 14. Conserve and sustainably use the oceans, seas and marine resources for sustainable development
Goal 15. Protect, restore and promote sustainable use of terrestrial ecosystems, sustainably manage forests, combat desertification, and halt and reverse land degradation and halt biodiversity loss
Goal 16. Promote peaceful and inclusive societies for sustainable development, provide access to justice for all and build effective, accountable and inclusive institutions at all levels
Goal 17. Strengthen the means of implementation and revitalize the global partnership for sustainable development

Source: United Nations, https://sdgs.un.org/2030agenda, (Access 3.1.2021).

---

[9] UN Department of Economic and Social Affairs, " Transforming Our World: the 2030 Agenda for Sustainable Development", https://sdgs.un.org/2030agenda (Access 3.1.2021).

These SDGs are illustrated with some symbols and short slogans as follows also.

Table 1. SDGs (Resource: UN, un.org, Access 3.2.2021)

The SDGs are tracked by tracking system which is named as "SDG Tracker"[10], and also reported globally[11] as well as nationally.[12]

SDG Tracker presents progress (as a free and open access publication) by using all available indicators from the Our World in Data database, based on official data from UN and other International Organizations. The new version of SDG Tracker was launched on 28th June 2018.

SDG Tracker says "….for many indicators data is available, but major data gaps remain".

By the way, how about the progress about the migration targets and indicators? Unfortunately, it is not obvious in SDGs. On this occasion, there is an absolute need of a new refugee indicator displacement in the Sustainable Development Golas (SDGs). Although the relationship between migration and development increasingly recognised, it remains under-explored.

Who brought up the issue (new refugee indicator displacement in the SDGs) and how ?

The need mentioned above is brought up by different parties and analysed also with some hints and even blueprints in terms of solution for this problematic. I please readers to pay attention to the preference of "problematic" instead of "problem". Because it is an issue of this kind, a

---

[10] SDG Tracker, "Measuring progress towards the SDGs", https://sdg-tracker.org/ (Access 3.1.2021)
[11] Sustainable Development Solutions Network, "Sustainable Development Report 2020", https://sdgindex.org/reports/sustainable-development-report-2020/ (Access 3.1.2021)
[12] The Presidency Strategy and Budget, "Turkey's Sustainable Development Goals 2nd VNR 2019", https://www.sbb.gov.tr/wp-content/uploads/2020/03/Susta%C4%B1nable-Development-Goals-Turkeys-2nd-Vnr_EN-WEB.pdf, (Access 3.1.2021)

globe of problems mixture intercorrelated, and seen as fractal geometric structure.

ODI: Briefings and Report

For example, as an independent and a global think tank, the Overseas Development Institute (ODI) - in a series of 12 policy briefings- has analysed the links between migration and development outcomes in key areas as follows: decent work, poverty, urbanisation, gender, education, health, social protection, water and sanitation, energy, citizenship, technology and climate change.

Each briefing explores how migration affects different kinds of development outcomes and, in turn, the achievement of the SDGs. It also offers pragmatic recommendations to ensure that migration is incorporated into the 2030 Agenda and contributes to positive development outcomes.[13] According to ODI,

"The 2030 Agenda is well placed to reflect and exploit the links between migration and development for three reasons. First, the 2030 Agenda is the first international development framework to include and recognise migration as a dimension of development. Second, migration interacts with all dimensions of development. The multi-disciplinary and cross-sectoral nature of the 2030 Agenda is a useful platform to assess the impact of migration and human mobility on a range of development issues. This is not just important in terms of problem analysis but also offers opportunities for finding policy solutions. Finally, and crucially, the 2030 Agenda is supported by the necessary political 'traction' in different member states and in the multilateral system. The impacts of migration can be felt at all stages of the journey – notably in both origin and host countries – and as such it interacts with different sectors, requiring coordination between multiple actors and enhanced coherence across policies. This kind of coordination is only possible with high-level buy-in, something the SDGs have already secured. Furthermore, the SDGs' multi-disciplinary nature increases the potential for multi-stakeholder collaboration".[14]

ODI says "The 2030 Agenda includes a number of targets which recognise the economic value of migrants including SDGs 4, 5, 8, 10, 16 and 17 (given in Table 2). In particular, target 10.7 – the cornerstone of migration

---

[13] ODI (Overseas Development Institution), "Migration and the 2030 Agenda for Sustainable Development", Swiss Agency for Development and Cooperation, 2018, p.5, https://www.odi.org/projects/2849-migration-and-2030-agenda-sustainable-development (Access 3.1.2021)
[14] ibid, p.5.

in the 2030 Agenda – calls for the facilitation of 'safe, regular and responsible migration' and the implementation of 'well-managed migration policies".[15]

Table 2. The targets that mention migration (Resource : ODI, 2018)

4.b	By 2020, substantially expand globally the number of scholarships available to developing countries in particular LDCs, SIDS and African countries, for enrolment in higher education, including vocational training and ICT, technical, engineering and scientific programmes in developed countries and other developing countries
5.2	Eliminate all forms of violence against all women and girls in the public and private spheres, including trafficking and sexual and other types of exploitation
8.7	Take immediate and effective measures to eradicate forced labour, end modern slavery and human trafficking and secure the prohibition and elimination of the worst forms of child labour, including recruitment and use of child soldiers, and by 2025 end child labour in all its forms
8.8	Protect labour rights and promote safe and secure working environments for all workers, including migrant workers, in particular women migrants, and those in precarious employment
10.7	Facilitate orderly, safe, regular and responsible migration and mobility of people, including through the implementation of planned and well-managed migration policies
10.c	By 2030, reduce to less than 3% the transaction costs of migrant remittances and eliminate remittance corridors with costs higher than 5%
16.2	End abuse, exploitation, trafficking and all forms of violence against and torture of children
17.18	By 2020, enhance capacity building support to developing countries, including for Least Developed Countries (LCDs) and Small Island Developing States (SIDS), to increase significantly the availability of high-quality, timely and reliable data disaggregated by income, gender, age, race, ethnicity, migratory status, disability, geographic location and other characteristics relevant in national contexts

Now let us cock an ear at ODI for the catching pinpoint:

"Outside these targets, however, the Agenda is silent on the broader contribution of migration to development outcomes. These omitted and 'indirect' links between migration and development are the focus of our work. Our analysis, which has explored the links between migration and 15 of the 17 SDGs, shows that migration is not a development 'problem' to be solved (as is the subtext of SDG 10.7), but a mechanism or a strategy that can contribute to the achievement of many of the goals. To do this, governments and other actors need to identify the multiple linkages between migration and different goals and targets (Table 3), while at the same time also recognising that migrants can also be vulnerable and should be considered under the general principle of 'leaving no one behind".[16]

In this study ODI has prepared a table including multiple linkages between migration and different golas and targets. Let us see those impacts of migration on different SDGs and targets in Tables 3.1 to 3.3.[17]

---

[15] ibid, p.6.
[16] ibid, p.6.
[17] ibid, p.10-12.

Table 3.1 The impact of migration on SDGs

Goal	Target	Briefing	Link with migration
1 NO POVERTY	1.a	Poverty	Remittances and other forms of diaspora financing can be mobilised to improve infrastructure, services and development in origin countries.
	1.a	Social protection	Labour migrants present an opportunity to increase the tax base, and a greater number of contributors to social insurance-type schemes leads to better risk pooling and financial sustainability.
	1.b	Poverty	Migration is a key poverty reduction strategy and can be included in policy frameworks.
	1.1, 1.2	Poverty	Migration is a powerful poverty reduction strategy, for migrants themselves and their families in origin countries.
	1.1	Education	If migrants have access to education, it can lead to higher incomes.
	1.1	Urbanisation	Rural to urban migration contributes to economic development in origin countries and poverty reduction for migrants themselves.
	1.3	Citizenship	Migrants lacking permanent residency and/or citizenship status may not be able to access social protection.
	1.3	Social protection	Labour migrants can be a particularly poor and vulnerable group, but often lack eligibility for legal social protection and/or are not effectively covered.
	1.3	Urbanisation	Due to lack of formal registration in the city, many (poor) internal migrants cannot access social protection systems.
	1.4	Poverty	Migration can help families in origin countries improve their wellbeing through increased income, consumption and resilience.
	1.4	Water	Managing water resources sustainably, and providing water, sanitation and hygiene services, can enable successful migration, playing an important role in reducing poverty for migrants.
	1.5	Climate change	The poor are the most vulnerable to climate change, and are also the people who will find it hardest to migrate.
2 ZERO HUNGER	2.2	Health	Migrants are a particularly vulnerable group but may not be reached by assistance programmes aimed at improving nutrition.
3 GOOD HEALTH AND WELL-BEING	3	Education	Education, particularly female education, has a strong impact on the future health outcomes of migrant students and their families.
	3	Poverty	Migration improves healthcare access and health outcomes for families in origin countries.
	3.1	Health	Migrants are vulnerable to poor health outcomes, yet find it difficult to access health-care services in transit and host countries; the services they can access are often sub-standard.
	3.3	Water	In origin countries, poor water, sanitation and hygiene services can contribute to health shocks that inhibit successful migration.
	3.8	Citizenship	Eligibility for health access is often tied to residency and/or citizenship status, with only some countries opening up (emergency) health care to all.
	3.8	Health	Internal migrants often work in the informal sector and aren't covered by insurance, including universal health coverage.
	3.8	Urbanisation	Internal migrants often end up in a city's informal sector and therefore invisible to universal health coverage programmes.

Table 3.2 The impact of migration on SDGs

Goal	Target	Briefing	Link with migration
4 QUALITY EDUCATION	4	Poverty	Migration helps improve education access and outcomes for families in origin countries, helping to reduce poverty.
	4.1	Citizenship	Eligibility for education is often tied to residency and/or citizenship status, which means that migrant children can be excluded.
	4.1, 4.3	Decent work	Primary, secondary and higher education is necessary for the attainment of decent work later in life - particularly that which demands highly skilled individuals.
	4.4	Urbanisation	Internal migrants often lack the skills and training required to access decent jobs in the city and as a result end up working in low-productivity jobs in the informal sector.
	4, 4.1, 4.2, 4.5, 4.7	Education	While migration helps improve both education access and quality for families in origin countries, migrant children in host countries are often excluded from quality education.
5 GENDER EQUALITY	5.2	Decent work	Foreign domestic work is a key area of employment for female labour migrants, but also one of the least protected in terms of exploitation and violation of rights.
	5.2	Gender	Migrant and refugee women and girls can experience violence at all stages of the migration process, especially during transit (e.g. at refugee camps) or in their host country (e.g. by an employer).
	5.3	Education	If migrant children are enrolled in education, they are better able to resist child, early and forced marriage and female genital mutilation, and host-country governments can more easily intervene.
	5.3	Gender	Girls facing harmful practices such as female genital mutilation or forced marriage may use migration as a means of escape.
	5.4	Social protection	Migrant women often lack regularised status or access to social insurance through their employer.
	5.4	Urbanisation	Many migrant domestic workers in cities are female. Actions that increase the value of domestic work would enhance the well-being, dignity and status of migrant workers.
6 CLEAN WATER AND SANITATION	6.1 6.2	Health	Large-scale movements of people can increase stress on fragile water supply systems in origin and host countries. This can lead to adverse health effects such as disease.
	6.1 6.2	Water	Migrants can face significant barriers in accessing water, sanitation and hygiene services, particularly when they are in transit or undocumented.
7	7	Energy	By moving, migrants can improve their access to affordable, reliable, renewable modern energy services.
8 DECENT WORK AND ECONOMIC GROWTH	8	Poverty	Migration and remittances can lead to economic growth, a reduction in unemployment and increased wages in origin countries.
	8	Social protection	Migration can be an important contribution to economic development in origin countries through remittances, investment and knowledge exchange.
	8.1	Decent work	Migration can contribute to economic growth across different 'migration spaces' (at host, in transit and at origin).
	8.1	Education	The extent of education access and quality are important drivers of economic growth and differences in growth rates between regions.
	8.2	Technology	High-skilled migrants contribute to innovation and increase productivity by conducting research and development, creating new products and improving existing products.
	8.5	Decent work	In host countries, high-skilled migration can create new jobs for natives through new businesses, but low-skilled migration can have a 'crowding out' effect.
	8.5	Gender	Female refugees and migrants may be prevented from working, experience de-skilling, or be confined to 'feminine' jobs which are often paid or valued less than other work.
	8.7	Gender	Female migrants (particularly irregular migrants and children) are at risk of forced labour, trafficking, and exploitation and abuse.
	8.8	Decent work	Labour migrants are disproportionately affected by violations of employment rights. Efforts must clearly establish whose responsibility it is to protect those rights, and ensure proper enforcement.
	8.5 8.8	Urbanisation	Low-skilled rural to urban migrants seeking better job opportunities in the city often end up working in precarious occupations in the informal economy.

Table 3.3 The impact of migration on SDGs

Goal	Target	Briefing	Link with migration
9 REDUCED INEQUALITIES	9	Poverty	Migration can foster innnovation in host countries through greater diversity, and in origin countries through social remittances, skills transfers and return migration.
	9.5	Technology	Migration can enhance the technological capabilities of natives in host countries who work directly with high-skilled migrants, and of those in origin countries working with diaspora networks.
10 REDUCED INEQUALITIES	10	Poverty	Migration can reduce global inequalities, among countries and people, as people migrate from low- to high-income countries, and send remittances back home.
	10.c	Urbanisation	Internal remittances to poor households are often sent through informal channels as poor internal migrants do not have access to bank accounts. Such services can be riskier and more expensive.
	10.1	Education	Access to education can reduce inequality through raising incomes and reducing poverty for migrants, and boosting growth rates and government revenues in host countries.
	10.2	Education	Education can improve the social, economic and political inclusion of migrant children, particularly if they are able to speak the majority language.
	10.4	Social protection	Labour migrants are often not eligible for social protection, nor do they take it up. If vulnerable groups are unable to participate in social protection, inequalities widen.
	10.7	Energy	To ensure safe and responsible migration, especially in transit, migrants need access to modern energy services.
	10.7	Technology	Digital apps and mobile technologies can facilitate migration and integration into host countries.
	10.7	Urbanisation	Some countries discourage internal migration for work, having a direct impact on migrants' well-being and on the host city and country economies.
11 SUSTAINABLE CITIES AND COMMUNITIES	11.1	Water	Providing water, sanitation and hygiene services to slums and informal areas can help reduce inequalities and strengthen social cohesion.
	11.1, 11.2	Education	Improving housing and infrastructure would assist refugee and migrant children in accessing education services and achieve strong learning outcomes.
	11.3	Urbanisation	If host countries are to maximise the benefits of migration, they must take into account the needs of poor internal migrants and enhance their well-being.
13 CLIMATE ACTION	13	Climate change	Migration is an adaptation strategy to climate change – both extreme and slow-onset changes. Policies and financial planning need to take these patterns into account.
16 PEACE, JUSTICE AND STRONG INSTITUTIONS	16	Citizenship	Lack of citizenship/permanent residency can prevent migrants from being full members of society and can lead to tensions and conflict.
	16	Gender	Irregular and young migrants, particularly girls, are at greater risk of violence, trafficking and sexual exploitation.
	16.1, 16.9	Health	Many migrants lack legal identity, yet such an identity is important to effectively plan and establish health support systems.
	16.2	Education	Providing financial support to families in an attempt to eliminate child labour, exploitation and trafficking will most likely boost education for migrant children.
	16.3	Citizenship	When migrants cannot obtain residency and/or citizenship status, they may struggle to get equal treatment within the justice system or access legal aid.
17 PARTNERSHIPS FOR THE GOALS	17	Education	Data pertaining to migration background and education level is not collected together. This information should be used to support vulnerable groups, and not for reporting to security-related institutions.
	17	Health	There are no international standardised approaches for monitoring the health of migrants. Such data would help understand migrant health needs.
	17.6	Technology	Enhancing technological sharing, transfer, dissemination and education between host and origin countries would ensure migration contributes to economic transformation.
	17.8	Urbanisation	There is only limited data on internal migration. Improving the evidence base would enable us to better understand the scale and impact of internal migration, and design better policies.

UNDP Studies and Global Compact and SDGs

UNDP works in about 170 countries and territories, helping to eradicate poverty, reduce inequalities and build resilience so countries can sustain progress. As the UN's development agency, UNDP plays a critical role in helping countries achieve the Sustainable Development Goals. It is in this context that UNDP is one of the key members that supports Member States to achieve the goals set in the Global Compact for Migration once adopted in December 2018.

As Global Co-lead / Co-ordinator, UNDP Migration&Displacement Policy and Programming; and Team Leader, Livelihoods and Economic Recovery Mr. Owen Shumba (after The High-level Political Forum (HLPF) which was held in the first half of 2019 in New York City which had the theme 'Empowering People and Ensuring Inclusiveness and Equality' and it reviewed several Sustainable Development Goals (SDGs) in depth, particularly those related to migration) says,

> "….in supporting Member States to implement the Global Compact for Migration, using the SDGs as our core framework and in partnership with other agencies, UNDP will concentrate on three main areas:
> i) Minimizing the adverse drivers and structural factors that compel people to leave their country of origin, including building resilience in crisis and post-crisis situations.
> ii) Creating conditions for migrants/diasporas to fully contribute to sustainable development in all countries.
> iii) Supporting conditions for sustainable reintegration (also linked to our work on the re/integration of internally displaced people and refugees).[18]

He adds that "However, SDG targets and indicators do not sufficiently address displacement. It is evident that lack of quality education, economic opportunities, inequality, climate change and governance combine to form the root causes of forced displacement.

> Together with our partners in the UN community, UNDP stands ready to support member states in addressing migration and displacement using the 2030 Agenda and the SDGs as frameworks with focus on:
> Compiling Voluntary National Reviews that address the challenges, lessons and concrete strategies on migration and displacement;
> Building the capacity of migrants, refugees and displaced people to cope, recovery and sustain their development gains in the medium and long term;
> Creating an enabling environment for sustainable re-integration;
> Integrating migration into development plans, national SDGs and harness the positive contributions of migrants;

---

[18] Owen Shumba, "A-turning-point-on-migration", https://www.undp.org/content/undp/en/home/blog/2018/A-turning-point-on-migration.html (Access 3.1.2021)

Addressing the root causes of forced displacement, be they poverty and inequality, climate change, governance or violent conflict".[19]

He concludes that "we cannot achieve the SDG targets by 2030 without investing in support to vulnerable populations such as refugees, internally displaced persons, migrants, and of course other groups such as women and people with disabilities. We need to ensure that they have a share in production, as well as any skills to counteract the impact the industrial revolution and surge in artificial intelligence bring with them, which may even deepen inequality.[20]

Recently a report tittled "Shaping the Trends of Our Time" was prepared and published by the United Nations Economist Network under the guidance of Elliott Harris, United Nations Assistant Secretary-General for Economic Development and Chief Economist.

This report examines some of the successes and failures of the past, with a view to identifying how our efforts must be reinforced and redirected to ensure that we achieve the full measure of the 2030 Agenda, and set the stage for an inclusive, sustainable and equitable future during the next 75 years. It elaborates five megatrends: climate change; demographic shifts, particularly ageing; urbanization; the emergence of digital technologies in the fourth industrial revolution; and inequalities. As it is emphasized in the report climate change has an exclusive importance within SDGs.[21]

In that sense, Owen Shumba adds that, "Climate change is exacerbating migration and displacement. UNDP will continue to support countries bringing about real and positive change towards resilient, zero carbon development, and climate change adaptation. We are supporting countries to eliminate barriers to this ambitious transition, by formulating a systemic, integrated approach through governance and policy frameworks, inclusive leadership, transparency systems, combining climate finance and Nationally Determined Contributions (NDC) objectives. We are now supporting countries to address the root causes of displacement and migration. UNDP is supporting peace, justice and strong institutions to end abuse, exploitation, trafficking and violence (SDG 16) through UN Action for Cooperation against Trafficking in Persons (UN-ACT) programme".[22]

Owen Shumba concludes that, "The HLPFs are important for the

[19] Owen Shumba, "Migration, displacement and the SDGs and the SDGs at High Level Political Forum", https://www.undp.org/content/undp/en/home/blog/2019/migrant--displacement-and-the-sdgs-at-the-high-level-political-f.html (Access 3.1.2021)
[20] ibid.
[21] UNDESA, Report of the UN Economist Network for the UN 75th Anniversary Shaping the Trends of Our Time, UN Publications, 2020, p.3.
[22] Shumba, ibid.

international community to renew the commitments to address both migration and displacement, using the 2030 Agenda and the Sustainable Development Goals as key frameworks. This should continue, but a way to strengthen the outcome must be charted soon".[23]

International Organisation for Migration (IOM) World Migration Report (WMR) 2020

In WMR 2020 which is prepared and published by IOM, some important issues are emphasized as follows:

" a) The unfortunate reality is that have been major migration and displacement events during the years 2018-2019 due to conflict, extreme violence, severe economic and political instability and also climate and weather-related hazards.

b) The scale of international migration increase in line with recent trends. The number of international migrants is estimated to be almost 272 million globally, with nearly two-thirds being labour migrants. This figure remains a very small percentage of the world's population (at 3.5%), meaning that the vast majority of people globally (96.5%) are estimated to be residing in the country in which they were born. However, the estimated number and proportion of international migrants already surpasses some projections made for the year 2050, which were in the order of 2.6 per cent or 230 million. That said, it is widely recognized that the scale and pace of international migration is notoriously difficult to predict with precision because it is closely connected to acute events (such as severe instability, economic crisis or conflict) as well as long-term trends (such as demographic change, economic development, communications technology advances and transportation access). We also know from long-term data that international migration is not uniform across the world but is shaped by economic, geographic, demographic and other factors resulting in distinct migration patterns, such as migration "corridors" developed over many years (see chapter 3 of this report for details). The largest corridors tend to be from developing countries to larger economies such as those of the United States, France, the Russian Federation, the United Arab Emirates and Saudi Arabia. This pattern is likely to remain the same for many years into the future, especially as populations in some developing subregions and countries are projected to increase in coming decades, placing migration pressure on future generations.[24]

In the Report complex and emerging migration issues ar given as a box

---

[23] ibid.
[24] IOM, World Migration Report 2020, Geneva-Switzerland, IOM, 2019, p.3.

(Table 4) as follows:[25]

Table 4. Complex&emerging migration

Highlights from Part II: Complex and emerging migration issues

- Migrants have made significant sociocultural, civic-political and economic contributions in origin and destination countries and communities, including by being important agents of change in a range of sectors (chapter 5).

- Immigrants tend to have higher entrepreneurial activity compared to natives. In countries such as the United States, migrants have disproportionately contributed to innovation (chapter 5).

- Migrants' inclusion in the receiving society relates to diverse societal/policy areas that are closely interdependent. Inclusion outcomes in one policy area – such as language, education, labour market inclusion, family reunification, political participation and naturalization – will likely impact others (chapter 6).

- There is a dynamic and complex relationship between migration and health that extends well beyond crisis events. Migration can lead to greater exposure to health risks but it can also be linked to improved health, especially for those seeking safety from harm (chapter 7).

- While the majority of children who migrate do so through safe migration processes as part of family units, many other child migrants lack effective protection from harm and face human rights violations at all stages of their journeys (chapter 8).

- The most recent global estimate for the total number of child migrants is approximately 31 million. There are approximately 13 million child refugees, 936,000 asylum-seeking children, and 17 million children who have been forcibly displaced inside their own countries (chapter 8).

- There is increasing evidence that the magnitude and frequency of extreme weather events are rising, and this is expected to increasingly affect migration and other forms of movement. While human mobility resulting from environmental and climate change is often framed along protection and security lines, understanding mobility as adaptation allows for migrants' agency to be part of the response equation (chapter 9).

- Migration status can significantly impact on migrants' ability to deal with crisis. Flexible immigration and visa policies help make it possible for migrants to keep themselves safe as well as recover from the impact of a crisis. Return is one, but not necessarily the primary, response option (chapter 10).

- The last two years have seen substantial change in the global governance of migration, principally in the formation of the United Nations Network on Migration and the two global compacts on refugees and migration. Although they are not legally binding, the two global compacts represent a near-universal consensus on the issues requiring sustained international cooperation and commitment (chapter 11).

As it is seen in Table 4, these comlex and emerging issues are analyzed in different chapters of the Report. All the issues handled are very much correlated with the SDGs. For example, investment in the field of migration and health supports social and economic development. Investment in monitoring and mitigating health risks is key to maintaining the health of migrants which, as a result, supports progress towards the Sustainable

---

[25] ibid, p.6.

Development Goals and global health targets.

IOM developed "The Global Migration Data Portal" in December 2017 as a one-stop access point for timely, comprehensive migration statistics and reliable information about migration data globally. A specific section shows how data can support United Nations Member States in achieving the migration-relevant Sustainable Development Goals and in implementing the Global Compact for Safe, Orderly and Regular Migration.

It should be emphasized that the 19th objective within the 23 objectives of Global Compact for Safe, Orderly and Regular Migration is written as follows: "Create conditions for migrants and Diasporas to fully contribute to sustainable development in all countries".[26]

A sample of inter-agency collaborations (DESA and IMO) in research projects on migration is Co-custody of [Sustainable Development Goal] indicator 10.7.2 on countries with well managed migration policies.

"A central goal of the Global Compact for Migration is to advance the important Sustainable Development Goal (SDG) on migration. This SDG, identified as SDG Target 10.7, calls on States to "facilitate orderly, safe, and responsible migration and mobility of people, including through implementation of planned and wellmanaged migration policies".72 The Initiative for Child Rights in the Global Compacts, a multi-stakeholder effort to highlight child migrant issues, identified several priority areas for making SDG Target 10.7 a reality for children".[27]

OCHA Global Humanitarian Overview Report 2021

According to Global Humanitarian Report 2021 prepared by UN Office for the Coordination of Humanitarian Affairs (OCHA), one of the recent trends and chalenges is related to migration. The report says *"The last decade saw the highest-ever number of people internally displaced by conflict and violence, with many locked in a state of protracted displacement. There are an estimated 51 million new and existing IDPs, and the number of refugees has doubled to 20 million".*[28]

Besides displacement, other global trends underlined in the report are correlated with SDGs as well:

COVID-19 has triggered the deepest **global recession** since the 1930s; **hunger** is on the rise; severe and frequent weather events and natural disasters are exacerbating chronic vulnerabilities; COVID-19 has shone a

---

[26] ibid, p. 297.
[27] ibid, p. 249.
[28] OCHA, Global Humanitarian Overview Report 2021, OCHA Publications, 2020, p.3.

spotlight on the full extent of **gender inequality** and women's and girls' exposure to gender-based violence (GBV), new **innovative** technologies offer the potential to improve humanitarian action; **collaboration** between humanitarian, development and peacebuilding efforts has increased during the pandemic etc.[29]

Conclusion

Based on all the information and discussions given in the sections above, a conclusion including some detections and some offerings may be summarized. Let us try to do that (also benefiting from the conclusions by ODI, IOM and OCHA in their Reports).

First of all, it must be said that migration is a powerful poverty reduction tool, which can contribute to the achievement of all SDGs.

Secondly, it is watched that the specific risks and vulnerabilities of migrants are often overlooked. For example, female migrants, who tend to work in less regulated and less visible sectors, are at greater risk of exploitation and abuse, including trafficking.

Pevehouse and Goldstein says "In addition to migration and refugees, a growing number of people - estimated at about 700,000 annualy – are trafficked across international borders against their will. They include both sex slaves and labor slaves, with each category including females and males, adults and children. Perhaps 20,000 of these people are trafficked to the United States annually".[30]

Ahead of deliberations on the Global Compact for Safe, Orderly and Regular Migration, the United Nations Agenda for Sustainable Development made mention of migration, although the connection between migration and the environment was not explicitly stated. That said, the Agenda for Sustainable Development and its related goals for 2030 have paved the way for linking migration and the environment in future frameworks.

Thirdly, migrants can contribute to the provision and delivery of services and to greater development in host countries.

Fourthly and unfortunately, the implementation of existing programmes of support for migrants is often weak.

Fifthly and filthy there are major data gaps. Also confusions about the differences between the elements of cycle (data-information-knowledge-wisdom cycle) is going on idio(ma)tically! Data or information oriented style is seen and preferred practically (: easily), instead of knowledge and gradually

[29] İbid, p.3.
[30] John C.V. Pevehouse and Joshua S. Goldstein, International Relations, Harlow- UK, 2021, p. 430.

wisdom oriented style. By the way did you see a coin which has only tails (practice), they are always head and tails (theory and practice) aren't they? It is known that information is processed data; while the knowledge is the output resulted from analysis and synthesis of information. Until now the issue was "what is done?". Wisdom begins at the end, asking and answering question of "what to do?". Let's wrap up the issue what i mean with two proverbs: "Knowledge without wisdom is like water in the sand (Guinean proverb)"; "It requires wisdom to understand wisdom: the music is nothing if the audience is deaf (Walter Lippman, an American writer)".

CHAPTER 5

REFUGEE POLICY OF NORTH ATLANTIC TREATY ORGANIZATION (NATO)

Dinçer Bayer*

Introduction

North Atlantic Treaty Organization (NATO) is an international organization[1] providing security for its members. NATO is an intergovernmental organization in which each member country maintains its sovereignty. All NATO decisions are taken jointly based on the agreement of each member country. Its members are states parties to the founding NATO Treaty. It was founded after the Second World War in 1949 and has been the most influential security organization all over the world.

By the Treaty, the parties agreed to consult where the territorial integrity, political independence or security of any of them has been threatened and accepted that an armed attack against one or more of them in Europe or North America should be considered an attack against all. The alliance (now comprising thirty states[2]) consists of a Council which is the supreme organ and on which all members are represented and a NATO parliamentary conference (the North Atlantic Assembly), which acts as an official consultative body.

The ending of the Cold War in 1991 brought about a variety of changes in the organization. While providing security for its members was remaining the first task for NATO, crisis response capability has started playing much more role in NATO's plans and activities. Ms. Sur asserts that; as people continue to flee conflicts and unrest which occur many places on the globe and look for new places to settle, as host countries grapple to accommodate a massive influx of refugees, and new conflicts erupt over strained resources, NATO's role has evolved from ensuring state security to assuring the security of people. Toward this end, the important role that the NATO plays in

* Asst. Prof. Dr. Piri Reis University, Maritime Higher Vocational School, dbayer@pirireis.edu.tr
[1] International organizations are institutions established by states by means of international treaties. (Shaw, M. N., (2008). International Law, Sixth Edition, Cambridge University Press, UK. pp 1309. ISBN-13 978-0-511-45559-9).
[2] https://www.nato.int/nato-welcome/index.html, 20.11.2020.

preventing statelessness and building stability in crisis-prone areas makes a strong NATO all the more necessary and pertinent today.

In 1994, the Partnership for Peace program of NATO was inaugurated, and this brings together NATO, international organizations and other states into a co-operative framework not only on military issues but also on crisis such as refugee issues. The Euro-Atlantic Partnership Council (EAPC) was established in 1997. There are currently 40 partner states work with NATO on a wide range of political and security-related issues. While the Partnership for Peace focuses upon practical, defense-related and military co-operation, the EAPC constitutes the forum for broad consultation on political and security issues. Countries participating in the partnership for peace sign a framework document, affirming the commitment to the preservation of democratic societies and the maintenance of the principles of international law, to fulfil in good faith the obligations of the UN Charter and the principles contained in the Universal Declaration of Human Rights and to respect existing borders[3].

NATO changed its strategic concept in 2010[4]. The Strategic Concept aimed NATO continues to be effective in a changing world, against new threats, with new capabilities and new partners. It reconfirmed the primary task of member nations to defend one another against attack, including against new threats to the safety of the citizens.

The new concept commits the NATO to prevent crises, manage conflicts and stabilize post-conflict situations, including by working more closely with NATO's international partners, most importantly the United Nations and the European Union. The NATO is firmly committed to the purposes and principles of the Charter of the United Nations, which affirms the primary responsibility of the Security Council for the maintenance of international peace and security. This affirmation shows the NATO's commitments on required actions for the security threatening refugee issues.

NATO is currently dealing with refugee issues for two different reasons. First is to provide security to its members, second is to accomplish its commitments to the UN in support of the peace and crisis- management requirements. In this chapter, NATO's policy and capabilities on refugee issues will be evaluated.

Concept of Terms: NATO Terminology

Some terms related with refugee, migrant or humanitarian issues are

---

[3] NATO has involved many peacekeeping and peace-enforcement operations under UN Charter stated as in Shaw, M. N, ibid., chapter 22, p. 1279.
[4] NATO Strategic Concept Document, Adopted by Heads of State and Government at the NATO Summit in Lisbon, 19-20 November 2010. NATO Public Diplomacy Division, Brussels.

included in the NATO Terminology Document[5]. Some of these terms are listed below.

Asylum-Seeker (NATO Agreed): A person who seeks safety from persecution or serious harm in a country other than his or her own and awaits a decision on the application for refugee status under relevant international and national instruments.

Evacuee (NATO Agreed): A person who has been ordered or authorized to move from a place of danger by competent authorities, and whose movements and accommodation are planned, organized and controlled by such authorities.

Evacuation (Preferred): The clearance of personnel, animals, or materiel from a given locality.

Humanitarian Assistance (HA) (Preferred): As part of an operation, the use of available military resources to assist or complement the efforts of responsible civil actors in the operational area or specialized civil humanitarian organizations in fulfilling their primary responsibility to alleviate human suffering.

Humanitarian Operations (HUMRO) (NATO Agreed): An operation specifically mounted to alleviate human suffering in an area where the civil actors normally responsible for so doing are unable or unwilling adequately to support a population. Related Term: Humanitarian Relief Operation (Preferred)

Refugee (NATO Agreed): Any person who, owing to well-founded fear of being persecuted for reasons of race, religion, nationality, membership of a particular social group or political opinion, is outside the country of his nationality and is unable or, owing to such fear, is unwilling to avail himself of the protection of that country, or who, not having a nationality and being outside the country of his former habitual residence, is unable or, owing to such fear, is unwilling to return to it[6]. Related Terms: Refugee Support Coordination Centre (RSCC) (NATO Agreed), Displaced Persons and Refugees (DPRE) (NATO Agreed).

NATO's Transformation for Having More Crisis Response Capability:

Euro-Atlantic Disaster Response Coordination Centre (EADRCC) was established in 1998 by the Euro-Atlantic Partnership Council (EAPC) as a

---

[5] https://nso.nato.int/natoterm/Web.mvc, (Access 20.10.2020.
[6] Convention relating to the Status of Refugees, 1951, as modified by the Protocol relating to the Status of Refugees, 1967

partnership tool of NATO's civil emergency planning and as one of the two basic elements of the EAPC policy on cooperation in the field of international disaster relief. The other, complementary element is the Euro-Atlantic Disaster Response Unit, a non-standing, multinational force of civil and military elements, deployable in the event of major natural or man-made disasters in a NATO member or partner country.

Initially, the EADRCC was extensively involved in coordinating humanitarian assistance efforts from EAPC countries that supported refugees during the Kosovo war in the late 1990s. Since then, however, the Centre has responded to many requests for assistance received mainly from states stricken by natural disasters but also to help with the consequences of chemical, biological, radiological or nuclear (CBRN) incidents, which includes terrorist attacks.

In case of civil emergencies, the EADRCC is NATO's principal response mechanism in the Euro-Atlantic area. The Centre forwards assistance requests to NATO and partner countries, which in turn respond by communicating their offers of assistance to the EADRCC and/or the affected country. It keeps track of the assistance offered (including assistance from other international organizations and actors), assistance accepted by the stricken country, delivery dates and assistance still required (or updates to the assistance requested), as well as the situation on the ground. This information is circulated to NATO and partner countries in the form of situation reports and is also published on the EADRCC website (http://www.nato.int/eadrcc).

All of the EADRCC's tasks are performed in close cooperation with the United Nations Office for the Coordination of Humanitarian Affairs (UN OCHA), which retains the primary role in the coordination of international disaster relief operations. The Centre is designed as a regional coordination mechanism, supporting and complementing UN efforts. Furthermore, its principal function is coordination rather than direction. In the case of a disaster requiring international assistance, it is up to individual NATO Allies and partners to decide whether to provide assistance, based on information received from the EADRCC.

The Centre is located at NATO Headquarters in Brussels, Belgium. It is staffed by persons from NATO and partner countries and members of NATO's International Staff. The Centre liaises closely with UN OCHA, NATO Military Authorities and other relevant international organizations. When a disaster occurs, the EADRCC can temporarily be augmented with additional personnel from NATO and partner delegations to NATO, or NATO's international civilian and military staff. In addition, the EADRCC has access to national civil experts that can be called upon to provide the

Centre with expert advice in specific areas in the event of a major disaster. Its crisis response and assistance coordination procedure is displayed in the Figure 1.

Figure 1. Euro-Atlantic Disaster Response Coordination Center's Crisis Response Procedure[7]

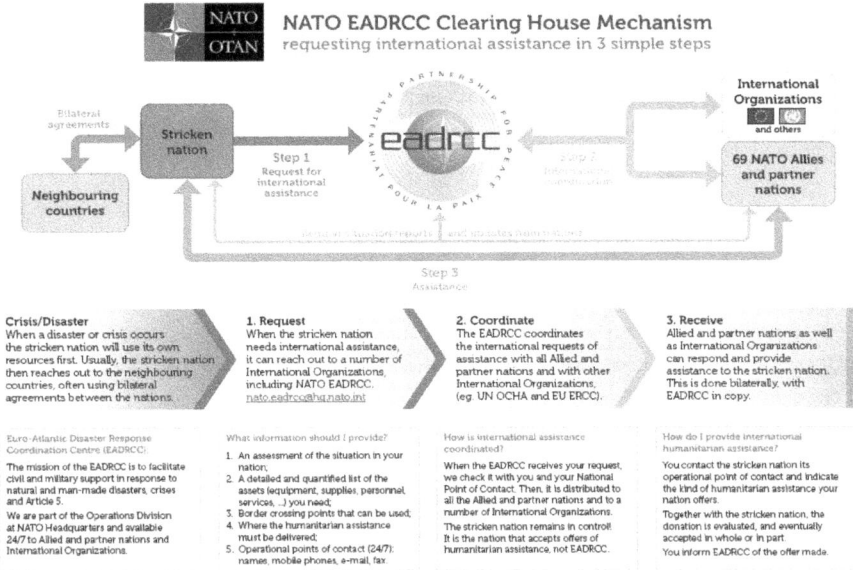

In January 2004, the North Atlantic Council, NATO's principal political decision-making body, widened the EADRCC's mandate to respond to assistance requests from the Afghan government in the case of natural disasters. Three years later, that mandate was extended to all areas where NATO is involved militarily. In 2009, the countries of the Mediterranean Dialogue[8] (MD) and those of the Istanbul Cooperation Initiative[9](ICI) were given direct access to the Centre, followed by other partners across the globe[10] in December 2011.

Today, NATO is not Just a Cold War Alliance:

According to the UN Refugee Agency, the world today is facing an

---

[7] Retrieved from; https://www.nato.int/nato_static_fl2014/assets/pdf/2020/4/pdf/200401-EADRCC-Requesting-assistance-in_3.pdf, (Access 24.11.2020).

[8] Algeria, Egypt, Israel, Jordan, Mauritania, Morocco and Tunisia.

[9] Six countries of the Gulf Cooperation Council were initially invited to participate. To date, four of these - Bahrain, Qatar, Kuwait and the United Arab Emirates - have joined. Saudi Arabia and Oman have also shown an interest in the Initiative.

[10] Afghanistan, Australia, Colombia, Iraq, Japan, the Republic of Korea, Mongolia, New Zealand and Pakistan.

unprecedented migrant crisis with 79,5 million forcibly displaced people worldwide, of which 26 million are refugees[11]. NATO has operations in many of the countries from which people are fleeing conflict, civil war, and unrest. NATO's presence is crucial to restoring stability to these regions and strengthening governance.

NATO has played a critical role in the past. In Sudan, for example, when pro-government Arab militia carried out ethnic cleansing of non-Arabs forcing thousands to flee, NATO helped the African Union (AU) expand its peacekeeping and humanitarian mission by coordinating the airlift of more than 30,000 AU troops into the region between June 2005 and December 2007.

One of the NATO's most significant, challenging, and longest missions has been in Afghanistan. Over the past eighteen years, NATO missions in Afghanistan have provided security, helped build the capacity of Afghan troops, and contributed to reconstruction and development work. Over the last few decades, conflict has forced millions of Afghans to flee. Yet those numbers could have been much higher had it not been for NATO's peacekeeping and rebuilding efforts in Afghanistan.

NATO can contribute to the efforts of the international community for maintaining peace, security and stability, in full coordination with other actors. Military means, although essential, are not enough on their own to meet the many complex challenges to the today's security. The effective implementation of a comprehensive approach to crisis situations requires nations, international organizations and non-governmental organizations to contribute to a concerted effort[12].

In Afghanistan, as in Bosnia and Kosovo, world society have learned that military power is no longer enough to ensure peace and may produce instabilities such as refugee flows and migrant problems. Peacekeeping has become at least as difficult as peacemaking.

In the new Strategic Concept agreed in 2010, the NATO committed itself to dealing with "all stages of a crisis – before, during and after" - an all-embracing principle that implies a greater role for cooperative security. Accordingly, the NATO is not only developing security partnerships with countries across the Mediterranean, the Gulf region, and even the Pacific area, but it is also reaching out to other fellow international organizations and non-governmental organizations that have mandates in such areas as institution-building, governance, development, and judiciary reform.

At the 2016 Summit in Warsaw, NATO decided to boost NATO's

---

[11] https://www.unhcr.org/figures-at-a-glance.html, (Access 22.10.2020).
[12] https://www.nato.int/cps/en/natolive/topics_51633.htm, (Access 20.11.2020).

resilience to the full spectrum of threats. They agreed seven baseline requirements for national resilience against which member states can measure their level of preparedness. One of the seven requirements was closely related with the capability on the refugee and migrant issues. This ability was to deal effectively with uncontrolled movement of people, and to de-conflict these movements from NATO's military deployments[13].

The 21st century has brought much uneasiness in many world regions primarily in Afghanistan, in Iraq and in Syria. Conflicts with different terrorist organizations such as Islamic State of Iraq and the Levant (ISIL) and other home-bred terrorism has become a brutal reality across many continents. Meanwhile, tensions rise as migrants seek refuge from conflict in countries that are struggling with the weight of ethnic and religious strife, demographic pressures and economic underperformance. These issues have been the main problems to be solved of the UN as being the main peace and security providing international organization.

NATO and UN Collaborations on Refugee Issues:

NATO and the United Nations (UN) share a commitment to maintaining international peace and security. The two organizations have been cooperating in this area since the early 1990s, in support of peace-support and crisis-management operations. The complexity of today's security challenges has required a broader dialogue between NATO and the UN.

Cooperation and collaborations efforts between NATO and UN are focused on the refugee issues. This has led to reinforced cooperation and liaison arrangements between the staff of the two organizations, as well as UN specialized agencies[14].

UN has sub-organizations/offices dealing with refugee and migrant issues. The primary institutions of those are the Organization for Migration (IOM), The United Nations High Commissioner for Refugees (UNHCR) and the UN Refugee Agency. UNHCR's primary purpose is to safeguard the rights and well-being of refugees[15]. The Office carries out its work in

---

[13] https://www.nato.int/cps/en/natohq/topics_49137.htm, (Access 20.11.2020).

[14] In October 2018, The Secretary-General of the United Nations and the Secretary General of the North Atlantic Treaty Organization, declared the consisted cooperation between the United Nations and NATO in support of the work of the United Nations in maintaining international peace and security, This cooperation will include, but are not limited to, countering the threat posed by improvised explosive devices; training and preparedness; capacity building and defense sector reform; the protection of civilians; advancing the women, peace and security, youth, peace and security and the children and armed conflict agendas; countering terrorism and preventing violent extremism; lessons learned, planning and support for contingencies; cyber defense; and operational coordination and support (https://www.nato.int/cps/en/natohq/official_texts_160004.htm?selectedLocale=en, (Access 20.11.2020).

[15] 2019 Global Report of UN Refugee Agency. Published by UNHCR. www.unhcr.org, (Access, 24.11.2020).

collaboration with many partners, including governments, regional organizations, and international and non-governmental organizations. UNHCR also cooperates with NATO on refugee issues.

NATO has also a close cooperation with the UN International Organization for Migration (IOM)16. In 2006 IOM and NATO's Supreme Headquarters Allied Powers, Europe (SHAPE) have signed an agreement to increase cooperation in natural disasters, complex emergencies and post conflict environments[17]. The agreement paved the way for an increased exchange of information and expertise at planning and operational levels to improve the capacity of both organizations to respond in times of humanitarian emergencies.

IOM coordinates the activities for refugee issues with means of 9 established regional offices. The regional offices oversee, plan, coordinate and support IOM activities within the region. Regional offices are responsible for project review and endorsement and provide technical support to country offices and international organizations.

The Regional Office Brussels- Belgium provides support to IOM offices within the Europe maintains liaison and partnerships with governments, development partners and civil society within the region; provides technical support to governments to develop national migration frameworks and strengthen migration governance systems. In addition to its regional functions, the Office coordinates IOM's relations and liaison with NATO. Therefore, NATO should coordinate all the activities related with refugee movements by means of the regional IOM Office Brussels.

NATO Operations and Missions Related with Refugee Movements:

NATO is an active and leading contributor to peace and security on the international stage. If diplomatic efforts fail, NATO in cooperation with other international organizations such as UN and European Union has the military capacity needed to undertake crisis management operations, alone or in cooperation with other organizations.

The Kosovo Refugee Crisis

Almost immediately after the inauguration of the EADRCC, the Centre was called upon to lend its support to the United Nations High

---

[16] Established in 1951, the International Organization for Migration is the leading inter-governmental organization in the field of migration. It works closely with governmental, intergovernmental and non-governmental partners. As of September 2016, IOM is an UN-related agency.
[17] https://www.iom.int/news/signing-agreement-between-iom-and-nato, (Access 22.10.2020).

Commissioner for Refugees (UNHCR) in coping with the emerging humanitarian crisis in and around Kosovo.

On 5 June 1998, the EADRCC received a request from the UNHCR to assist it by moving urgently needed relief items. In response to this request, 16 flights airlifted 165 tons of relief items from Sarajevo to Tirana.

With the lesson learned from The Kosovo refugee crisis, the EADRCC responsibilities were broadened along four major areas of activity, namely acting as a focal point for humanitarian assistance for all EAPC nations; coordinating requests and offers of assistance; providing support to the UNHCR; and keeping contacts NATO Military Authorities (NMAs) and others.

In March 2004, NATO troops evacuated 1000 people from their homes in Kosovo. The UN Refugee Agency Belgrade closely coordinated all the aid campaign with NATO to receive anyone fleeing the restive province for Serbia. The UN refugee agency in Serbia coordinated the efforts of receiving people fleeing the violence occurred in Kosovo, in addition to the more than 1,000 who had already been evacuated by NATO.

Influx of Refugees in Serbia

The Republic of Serbia experienced a significant influx of refugees in 2015. These refugees, mainly from Syria and Afghanistan, were transiting Serbia directed to Hungary and Croatia following the migrant routes towards north and western Europe. Since the beginning of 2015 more than 500.000 people have entered Serbia from the Republic of Macedonia[18]. The flow of new refugees was estimated between 4.000 - 5.000 people per day on this route. Many of them were women and children.

Due to the constant arrival of refugees transiting through the country, the Government of Serbia has decided to open an additional reception centre in Bujanovac, some 30km north of Presevo. Due to the overstretched national capacities and in light of the upcoming winter season additional humanitarian assistance was needed necessary. In accordance with the procedures, EADRCC has received a request for assistance from the Republic of Serbia on 17 December 2015. After that time, NATO provided Serbia Government the required amount of support to ease the refugee influx until the date of 12 September 2016.

Influx of Syrian Refugees in Turkey and Jordan

Due to the long-standing war in Afghanistan, the ongoing instability in

---

[18] https://natohqgeo.maps.arcgis.com/apps/Cascade/index.html?appid=f5c32302653b47578ed389561 a1ae993, (Access 22.10.2020).

Iraq since the 2001 Gulf Crisis, and the ongoing civil war in Syria since 2011, there is an immigration from South Asia and the Middle East region to Europe. Turkey, being a transit country for migrants and migration is the country most affected by this incident. For example, Turkey has hosted 4.5 million Syrian refugees and had difficulty in handling the situation[19].

On 13 April 2012, Turkey requested international assistance through the NATO Euro-Atlantic Disaster Response Coordination Centre (EADRCC) in the context of the increasing flow of Syrian refugees in the country. Turkey requested financial support, field hospitals, and accommodation equipment.

Events in Syria have resulted in a flow of Syrian refugees into Turkey and refugee camps have been set up on the Turkish side of the Syrian border. Turkey is putting every effort to meet the needs of the Syrian refugees to the extent possible making full use of its means and capabilities. However, upon the considerable increase in number of refugees, the Turkish authorities have decided to accept offers by the international community to share the burden. By the end of 2012, 7 Allied and partner nations had offered financial and in-kind support for the 150 000 refugees accommodated in 14 camps in Turkey.

The armed conflict in Syria resulted in a large number of Syrian citizens seeking refuge and shelter in Jordan. On 6 September 2012, Jordan requested international assistance to help with the build-up and running of the Za'atri refugee camp. At the end of 2012, some 174 000 Syrian refugees were registered or assisted in Jordan. Almost 50 000 of them lived in the Za'atri camp. 25 Allied and partner nations provided support to the NATO coordinated humanitarian operations.

Internally Displaced Persons (IDP) Crisis in Iraq

Hundreds of thousands of civilians fled in Iraq from advances of marauding fighters of the so-called "Islamic State of Iraq and Levant" (ISIL/Daesh) in the year 2014. With the humanitarian situation deteriorating the Government of Iraq requested international assistance on 19 August 2014 to cope with the rapidly increasing number of internally displaced persons (IDPs). Iraq requested accommodation equipment and subsistence for IDPs living in tented camps.

According to UN estimates, more than 2 million people had been displaced at the end of 2014 and were in need of humanitarian assistance. Till the end of 2014, 32 Allied and partner nations of NATO had provided in-kind or financial support to Iraq.

---

[19] According to the Turkish Authorities, there are 3.5 million registered and 1 million unregistered of Syrian refugees in Turkey. https://multeciler.org.tr/turkiyedeki-suriyeli-sayisi/, (Access 05.07.2019).

NATO's Aegean Sea Refugee Operations:

NATO is currently operating in Afghanistan and in the Mediterranean. Furthermore, NATO is assisting with the response to the refugee and migrant crisis in Europe. It also carries out disaster relief operations and missions to protect populations against natural, technological or humanitarian disasters. NATO is also providing support to assist with the consequences of this humanitarian crisis[20].

The refugee and migrant crisis, caused by conflict and instability in Afghanistan, Iraq and Syria effected Southern Europe which covers the NATO's southern borders, is being fueled by human trafficking and criminal networks.

In 2015, movements of migrants and refugees especially from Syria destined to reach the European countries over the Aegean Sea and through the Greece increased. Main nationalities arrived in Greece in the year 2015 by sea from Syria were 476 000, from Afghanistan were 206 000 and from Iraq were 87 000 according to data collected by UN International Office of Migrants staff on the Greek islands. 67,415 migrants and refugees reached the Greek islands only in one month in January 2016[21].

Migrants and refugees were also getting die at sea in 2015 and 2016. For example, on 7 March 2016 at least 25 migrants were reported drowned in the waters separating Turkey and Greece, bringing the number of fatalities in the Mediterranean to an estimated 443 in 2016, according to IOM's Missing Migrants Project. The five deadliest days on the Aegean between the September 2015 and January 2016 were as follows:

September 20, 2015. There were three incidents with a total of 54 deaths in the Aegean. One shipwreck was off the coast of Lesbos, killing 26, while another 26 were killed after their boat collided with a ferry off the Turkish coast.

October 28, 2015. There were 10 incidents in the Aegean, with a total of 78 deaths. They included two shipwrecks with a total of 43 deaths off Lesbos, and 19 off Kalymnos. Some 13 bodies were washed up on the shores of Lesbos in the following days, indicating there were even more migrants lost at sea.

January 21, 2016. There were three incidents in the Aegean with a total of 76 deaths, including two major shipwrecks. The Hellenic Coast Guard reported 44 deaths off the coast of Kalymnos, and a further 24 died sailing

---

[20] https://www.nato.int/cps/en/natohq/topics_128746.htm, (Access 20.11.2020).
[21] https://www.iom.int/news/mediterranean-migrant-arrivals-2016-141141-deaths-444, (Access 22.10. 2020).

to Lesbos.

January 28, 2016. One incident off the coast of Samos killed at least 41 migrants.

January 30, 2016. One incident killed 39 migrants on route to Lesbos.

According to NATO assessment, Europe had faced the greatest refugee and migrant crisis since the end of the Second World War[22]. In February 2016, on the request of Germany, Greece and Turkey, NATO decided to join international efforts in dealing with this refugee and migrant crisis. NATO has deployed a maritime force in the Aegean Sea to conduct reconnaissance, monitoring and surveillance of illegal crossings, in support of Turkish and Greek authorities and the EU's refugee control agency Frontex. By deploying its crisis response forces in the Aegean Sea, NATO contributed to the broader international efforts to stem illegal trafficking and illegal migration in the Aegean Sea, through intelligence, surveillance and reconnaissance in the Aegean Sea and at the Turkish-Syrian border.

NATO's standing naval forces are integrated into the NATO Response Force and provide the NATO with a continuous presence at sea. NATO's standing naval forces consist of four groups. These multinational forces regularly carry out patrols, exercises and port visits, work with partners, and can be rapidly deployed in times of tension or crisis. Therefore, they are the most suitable forces available to be deployed especially for the operations for cutting the sea lines of movement in case of the refugee flows. They also supported the NATO's Aegean deployment – helping to cut lines of illegal migration between Greece and Turkey[23].

NATO maritime forces are deployed in the Aegean Sea to contribute critical, real-time information to Greece and Turkey, as well as to Frontex, in light of the ongoing humanitarian crisis. NATO's Standing NATO Maritime Group 2 (SNMG2) is conducting reconnaissance, monitoring and surveillance of illegal crossings in the territorial waters of Greece and Turkey, as well as in international waters with its maritime and air assets. It is sharing whatever relevant information it finds with the Greek and Turkish coast guards and authorities. Greece and Turkey will only be operating in their own territorial waters and airspace. NATO is also sharing this information in real-time with Frontex so that it can take even more effective action. Since NATO's ships are larger than Frontex vessels, NATO sensors and radars have a broader reach and complement Frontex assets.

The purpose of NATO's deployment is to assist its Allies and Frontex in

---

[22] NATO's Deployment in the Aegean Sea, NATO Fact Sheet, Public Diplomacy Division (PDD) – Press & Media Section, October 2016.
[23] https://www.nato.int/cps/en/natohq/news_162393.htm?selectedLocale=en, (Access 24.11.2020).

carrying out their duties in the face of the crisis. In accordance with international law, all ships that sail, including NATO ships, have to rescue people in distress at sea. Allied vessels will live up to their national responsibility to assist.

The activity has been performed using part of the standing naval group assets, significantly reinforced by additional ships provided by NATO Allies. On average, there have been around six ships involved in the Aegean. Aegean operations are controlled and commanded by NATO Maritime Command (MARCOM), Northwood, United Kingdom. These are multinational, integrated maritime forces made up of vessels from various NATO countries. These vessels are permanently available to NATO to perform different tasks ranging from exercises to operational missions. They function according to the operational needs of the NATO, therefore helping to maintain optimal flexibility. Their composition varies and they are usually composed of between two and six ships from as many NATO member countries.

For dealing with the refugee and migrant crisis in the Aegean Sea, NATO is cooperating with the UN and EU, in full compliance with international law and the UN laws of the sea. NATO has established arrangements enabling direct links with UN and Frontex agency of the EU at the operational and tactical levels. This allows the exchange of liaison officers and the sharing of information in real-time. NATO ships are providing real-time information to the coastguards and relevant national authorities of Greece and Turkey, as well as to Frontex, helping them in their efforts to tackle this crisis.

Many ships from different NATO nations have participated in NATO's activities in the Aegean Sea. By using the information collected by NATO ships, Greece, Turkey and other international agencies are taking more effective action to break the business model of human traffickers and save lives. According to the statistics recorded by NATO, the number of migrants crossing the Aegean Sea has decreased significantly[24]

Conclusion

As the locations and the volume of the refugee and migrant crisis occurred Eurasia in the last 30 years were evaluated, it has been seen that NATO had always been in the front line of the refugee and migrant crisis. NATO presented solidarity and paid efforts to ease the results of refugee movements and to cut the lines of human smuggling and humanitarian disasters.

NATO which actually founded under the ideologic ideas of preventing war in the cold war era successfully transformed itself to the new era of human security and new types of crisis. NATO's new concept commits the

---

[24] NATO's Deployment in the Aegean Sea, ibid., p. 1.

NATO to prevent crises, manage conflicts and stabilize post-conflict situations, including by working more closely with NATO's international partners, most importantly the United Nations and the European Union. The NATO is firmly committed to the purposes and principles of the Charter of the United Nations, which affirms the primary responsibility of the Security Council for the maintenance of international peace and security. This affirmation shows the NATO's commitments on required actions for the security threatening refugee issues.

NATO is currently dealing with refugee issues for two different reasons. First is to provide security to its members, second is to accomplish its commitments to the UN in support of the peace and crisis- management requirements.

When the refugee issues come on the agenda, NATO cooperate with the UN agency and institutions. The agreements between NATO and UN cover the increasing the cooperation in natural disasters, complex emergencies and post conflict environments. The cooperation also paved the way for an increased exchange of information and expertise at planning and operational levels to improve the capacity of both organizations to respond in times of humanitarian emergencies.

NATO is an active and leading contributor to peace and security on the international stage. If diplomatic efforts fail, NATO in cooperation with other international organizations such as UN and European Union has the military capacity needed to undertake crisis management operations, alone or in cooperation with other organizations. New investments in NATO that focus on stabilizing conflict areas, modelled on NATO's current peacekeeping and capacity-building missions in places like Kosovo and Iraq, is certainly a better approach to reducing the influx of refugees and migrants instead of inhumane measures of detention, deportation and family separations.

CHAPTER 6

NATO AND THE CURRENT REFUGEE CRISIS: PROSPECTS AND CHALLENGES

Adnan Seyaz[*]

Introduction

North Atlantic Treaty Organization (NATO) is a Cold War product as a counterweight to the Soviet Union. Since its establishment in April 1949, NATO has been a collective defense organization against external threats. Following the Second World War, twelve countries[1] came together to prevent a third world war and signed the North Atlantic Treaty in Washington. Promoting stability and well-being in the North Atlantic area and safeguarding the freedom, common heritage, and civilization of the member countries were stated as the mandate of the organization.[2]

Almost 70 years later, today NATO consists of 30 members and has conducted missions in broad geography including Asia, Africa, North America along with Europe. These missions included air campaigns and disaster responses such as earthquake relief assistance in Pakistan. Disaster responses' existence in NATO operations history marked a redefinition of NATO's role ranging from military threats to non-conventional security challenges including counter-terrorism and societal and political instability.[3] Discussion on the Post-Cold War role of NATO paved the way to a new Strategic Concept and it has resulted in redrawing the goals and mission of the organization. These Post-Cold War strategic concepts contained a wider security area since security challenges that NATO faces are not the same as that of the Cold War Era. Aggression against the territory of a member state is no longer the only threat to the security of the Alliance. On the contrary, security threats to the Alliance are also coming from social, political, and economic instabilities in the close neighborhood.[4]

The inclusion of the migration within the NATO security preoccupation

---

[*] Ph.D. Faculty Member, Kirklareli University, Turkey, Faculty of Economics and Administrative Sciences,
[1] Founding members are the USA, Canada, the UK, France, Denmark, Portugal, Italy, Norway, Belgium, the Netherlands, Luxemburg, Iceland.
[2] Antonia-Maria Sarantaki, "Frontex and Nato: A New Partnership in the Making", Hellenic Foundation for European and Foreign Policy, Working Paper No 100/2019, January 2019, p. 5.
[3] Ibid.
[4] Margherita Bianchi, Guillaume Lasconjarias, and Alessandro Marrone, "Projecting Stability in NATO's Southern Neighbourhood", NDC Conference Report, No. 03/17 – July 2017.

has begun in this context just after the end of the Cold War. Manfred Wörner, NATO Secretary-General (1988-1994), became the first person to bring the migration problem to the North Atlantic Assembly as a threat to the territorial integrity of alliance members.[5] Thirty years after this speech, today, migration remains high on the agenda especially since the beginning of the Libyan and Syrian Civil Wars. Increasing numbers of people are crossing the borders in search of better economic and social conditions while millions of people escape from violence, war, human rights violations, and natural disasters. This chapter focuses on the role of NATO within the current refugee crisis. NATO's adaptation to the new security challenges will be dealt with to explore the significance of the refugee problem within this context. The process beginning with the end of the Cold War, when the migration issue entered into the NATO security preoccupation, is going to be analyzed with an emphasis on the crisis of the last decade.

Refugee, Refugee Crisis and NATO's Position

The refugee concept came to be used for all displaced persons in a broad sense generally within a political perspective. In recent years, especially, huge flows of people from a few countries fostered this understanding and the process came to be known as *the refugee crisis*. However, the United Nations High Commission on Refugees has a clarified definition of a refugee:

> "A refugee is someone who has been forced to flee his or her country because of persecution, war or violence. A refugee has a well-founded fear of persecution for reasons of race, religion, nationality, political opinion or membership in a particular social group. Most likely, they cannot return home or are afraid to do so. War and ethnic, tribal and religious violence are leading causes of refugees fleeing their countries."[6]

The refugee crisis, on the contrary, came to be used as a political concept and known with the huge flows of people in recent years.[7] Civil wars and humanitarian crises within just five countries, Syria-Venezuela-Afghanistan-South Sudan-Myanmar, caused flows of people across the border and constituted more than half of the total number. This is an enormous problem

---

[5] NATO, "Address given at the 36th Annual Session of the North Atlantic Assembly", Speech by Secretary General Manfred Wörner, 1990,
https://www.nato.int/cps/en/natohq/opinions_23706.htm?selected Locale=en (Access 07.10.2020).
[6] "What is a refugee", https://www.unrefugees.org/refugee-facts/what-is-a-refugee/ (Access 08.10.2020).
[7] According to UNHCR definitions the main difference in this case is crossing an international border. Those who have been forced to flee their home but never cross an international border are internally displaced persons (IDPs). Poeple how have fleed their country and seek sanctuary in another country by applying for asylum, the right to be recognized as a refugee and receive legal protection and material assistance, are sylum seekers.

in human history that was not experienced since the Second World War. Then, over 12 million people have fled their hometowns. Today, the problem which is called a refugee crisis includes much more than this. Especially with the beginning of the Syrian Civil War, millions of Syrians migrated to neighboring countries. Since 2014, the Republic of Turkey has been hosting the largest number of refugees[8] under the UNHCR's mandate in the World.[9] The recent crisis in different parts of the world enormously increased the number of UNHCR concerned population[10] to almost 86 million (2019), which was almost 36 million in 2012.[11]

Graphic 1. UNHCR Concerned Population

UNHCR Concerned Population

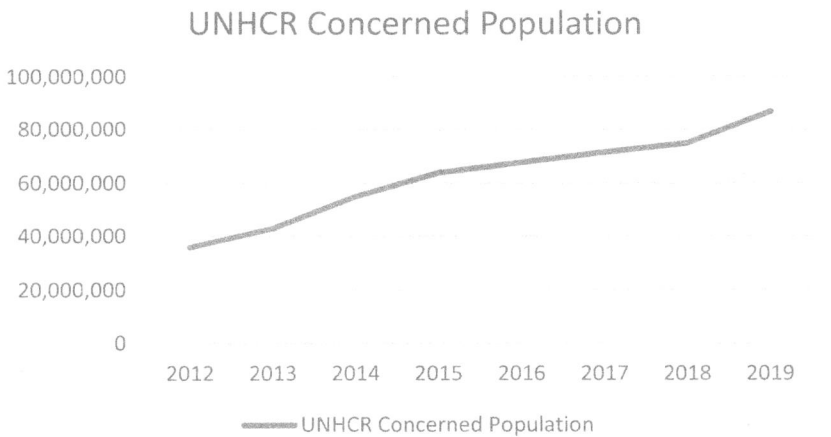

Source: "Populations, Global Focus: UNHCR Operations World Wide", the UNHCR

The world witnessed high media coverage of migrants only after the Syrian Civil War caused millions of migrants to flow towards European countries' territorial borders. Beginning in 2012 Syrian migrants started to flow to the territorial borders of Turkish, NATO borders indeed. The Turkish government's declaration that an open-door policy, inspired by the EU Temporary Protection Directive, will be applied to these migrants meant

---

[8] Turkey defines these people as under 'temporary protection' and officially does not name them as refugees depending on the 1967 additional Protocol Relating to the Status of Refugees, which brought new regulations in addition to 1951 Geneva Convention Relating to the Status of Refugees. Alan Makovsky, "Turkey's Refugee Dilemma: Tiptoeing Towards Integration", Center for American Progress, 13 March 2019.

[9] "Turkey, Global Focus: UNHCR Operasions World Wide", the UNHCR https://reporting.unhcr.org/turkey (Access 08.10.2020).

[10] The UNHCR concerned population includes refugees, asylum seekers, IDPs, returned IDPs, returned refugees, stateless and others of concern.

[11] "Populations, Global Focus: UNHCR Operasions World Wide", the UNHCR https://reporting.unhcr.org/population (Access 08.10.2020).

that the migrants would also reach easily to the European Union borders.[12] Particularly Greece and the Western Balkan countries had to cope with huge flows of migrants while Austria and Germany had to act since the former is a gate to the latter, which is the destination country for many of them. Although few years had passed since the beginning of the crisis NATO had stayed indifferent to the problem by 2015.[13] However, this crisis has the potential to destabilize Southern European countries which are either members or within the process of membership through MAP (Membership Action Plan) or IPAP (Individual Partnership Action Plan).[14] Moreover, NATO was not inexperienced in supporting civil emergencies.

On the contrary, NATO held relief and emergency missions in many cases such as Hurricane Katrina (August 2005)[15] in the USA, the earthquake in the Kashmir region of Pakistan (2005)[16], floods (2010)[17] in Pakistan, and so on. That is why NATO had to take action just after the refugee crisis stroke especially in South European countries. This argument may recall military operations experienced by NATO, however, that is not exactly my claim. NATO could provide logistics and necessary personnel to maintain stability in critical regions. It was also possible for NATO to work with the UNHCR in transferring the refugees to safe areas, offering field hospitals, and emergency housing.[18] European countries that faced the bitter face of human flows might call NATO to help. They are entitled to do it, indeed. Turkey, as a NATO member that felt pressure most together with Greece, called both the EU and NATO to provide stability in the region.[19] But, her voice was not heard enough in Brussels. Such a move could give meaning to the changing role of NATO and display a characterwise stance in the Post-Cold war process at earlier times.

Refugee Crisis and Problems for the Future of NATO

The 1990s witnessed a discussion on the role of the Alliance. While some

[12] Barbora Olejarova, "The Great Wall of Turkey: From the Open-Door Policy to Building Fortresses", **Polish Borderland Studies**, Vol. 6, No. 2, 2018, p. 121.
[13] Judy Dempsey, "NATO's Absence in the Refugee Crisis", 22 October 215, p. 1 https://carnegieeurope.eu/strategiceurope/61710 (Access 05.10.2020).
[14] Within MAP, there is only one country nowadays: Bosnia and Herzegovina; besides accession to the organization governed by IPAP through which Serbia, Ukraine, Georgia, Armenia, Azerbaijan and Kazakhistan are conducting their own relations seperately.
[15] NATO, "Hurricane Katrina", https://shape.nato.int/page139114921.aspx (Access 07.10.2020).
[16] NATO, "Eathquake Relief in Pakistan", https://shape.nato.int/page139125934.aspx (Access 07.10.2020).
[17] NATO, "NATO concludes airlift operations in support of the flood victims in Pakistan", 25 November 2010 https://www.nato.int/cps/en/natolive/news_68994.htm (Access 08.10.2020).
[18] Judy Dempsey, op. cit.
[19] Josh Lowe, "Germany and NATO call on NATO for Help with Refugee Crisis", Newsweek, 02 September 2016 https://www.newsweek.com/germany-merkel-turkey-davutoglu-call-nato-refugee-crisis-424430 (Access 11.10.2020).

argued that it is a mission-accomplished situation[20], some others foresaw a different future role for NATO. September 11 attacks and *the war on terrorism* provided a meaningful reason for the existence of the Alliance. In the following years, Russia came to the stage once more as the most significant 'threat' to the Alliance and caused discussions on the possibility of a new Cold War.

However, although Russian intervention in Georgia and the annihilation of Crimea in March 2014 increased the importance of the Alliance, NATO found herself within the discussions mostly voiced by the USA. Trump's inauguration witnessed such a crisis out of which two main points can be stated. The first one is about the way how Trump does politics. His way of creating a person to person relations left long-lasting principles of American foreign policy outside the agenda. Discussions of Putin's effect over the US presidential elections together with presidents' good personal relations after Trump's inauguration left NATO members in a shock when Trump suggested that he would not defend all its allies from attack.[21]

The second one is based on the members' commitment to increase their defense spending to reach 2% of their GDP by 2024. Trump is forcing European leaders to spend more on defense and he does not seem to approve of NATO's intensive involvement in the refugee crisis. Merkel's border policies irritated many European countries and the lack of solution directed them to NATO for protection from migrants.

The refugee crisis has another crisis embedded in it: the terrorist threat. Instability in the southern neighborhood of NATO caused a migrant influx to both NATO and the EU borders. However, while thousands of people are crossing land and sea borders of the organization, it is not possible to have proper border control and inspect them in person. Addressing this point NATO Secretary-General stated in 2016 that this is the greater challenge to the Alliance security since the end of the Cold War.[22] Russia's aggressive rise in world politics, the international terrorism addressing European capitals together with the regional instability in the MENA (the Middle East and North Africa) region created the most serious threat to the Alliance.

Countering such a challenge necessitated taking considerable steps and at the Warsaw Summit, NATO set her goals as projecting stability in the southern neighborhood. NATO had already engaged in the region through capacity building activities in Jordan and Tunisia, launching maritime security

---

[20] Timothy Andrews Sayle, **Enduring Alliance: A History of NATO and the Postwar Global Order,** London, Cornell University Press, 2019, pp. 191-215.
[21] Matt Peterson, "NATO in the Migrant Crisis", The Atlantic, 06 July 2018
https://www.theatlantic.com/membership/archive/2018/07/nato-in-the-migrant-crisis/564596/
(Access 12.10.2020).
[22] The Secretary General's Annual Report 2016, NATO, March 2017, p. 6.

operation Sea Guardian in the Mediterranean Sea, and the establishment of the Joint Force Command Naples as a hub to coordinate intelligence and contribute to the activities in the southern neighborhood.[23] As it is seen it was crucial, first of all, to agree on both strategic directions (East and South) were equally important for the security of the Alliance. But, this is only the first step in *projecting stability*. To put these objectives into practice the North American and European Allies should have a similar understanding of security in the MENA region. However, the European Allies themselves have divergency in their strategy towards unstable territories of the MENA region. That is why, NATO experienced immobility in taking further important steps due to the adverse interests of the Alliance members and the lack of state control in certain countries such as Libya, Syria, and Yemen.

Libyan case can be taken as the main example of the convergence of interests in the region. When the upheaval emerged in Qaddafi's Libya in 2011, it was supposed that the Europeans would assume a leadership role for the stability in the country. On the contrary, when the Paris Coalition (the US-France-Britain) led the operation to topple the Qaddafi regime other NATO allies such as Turkey strongly criticized their action.[24] Although UNSC's 17 March Resolution made Turkey reconsider her stance in the Libyan case, the crisis in the country was not effectively addressed by Europe neither through the EU mechanisms nor the NATO or any ad hoc format. Lastly, by January 2020, Turkey began to deploy critical equipment to the country to support the government recognized by the UN. The Turkish presence in the country generally attached a maritime agreement, a product of the Blue Homeland Doctrine[25] of Turkey, between two countries to secure access to resources and maritime boundaries in the Eastern Mediterranean. The Government of National Accord, recognized by the international community and the UN, achieved a phenomenal success against the LNA in 2020. Thus, the Libyan case showed us that since NATO allies did not have a clear stance and pursued their national interests, competition prevailed over cooperation in the MENA region. This factor prevented NATO from creating an enduring stance in the refugee crisis.

NATO's Involvement in Refugee Crisis

It was a very late date when NATO responded to calls from Germany, Greece, and Turkey in February 2016. By the time Turkey had already become the world's largest refugee host country in 2014 and hosted 2.733.044

---

[23] Bianchi, op. cit., p. 1.
[24] Burak Bilgehan Özpek and Yelda Demirağ, "Turkish foreign policy after the 'Arab Spring': from agenda-setter state to agenda-entrepreneur state", **Israel Affairs**, Vol. 20, No. 3, 2014, pp. 336-337.
[25] Esra Yalçınalp and Emre Temel, "Mavi Vatan nasıl doğdu? Doktrinin mimarları Cem Gürdeniz ve Cihat Yaycı anlatıyor", BBC Türkçe, 10 September 2020 https://www.bbc.com/turkce/haberler-turkiye-54096105 (Access 14.10.2020).

Syrians out of which 256.300 were in refugee camps by June 2016.[26] Within Greece, there were almost 50 thousand Syrian refugees who were stuck there after the closure of the Balkan route. Strict border controls and difficulty of moving through a few land borders directed refugees to the Mediterranean Sea where 2600 of them died while trying to reach Greek islands within the first half of 2016.[27]

Map I. Arrivals by Sea, 2015-2016

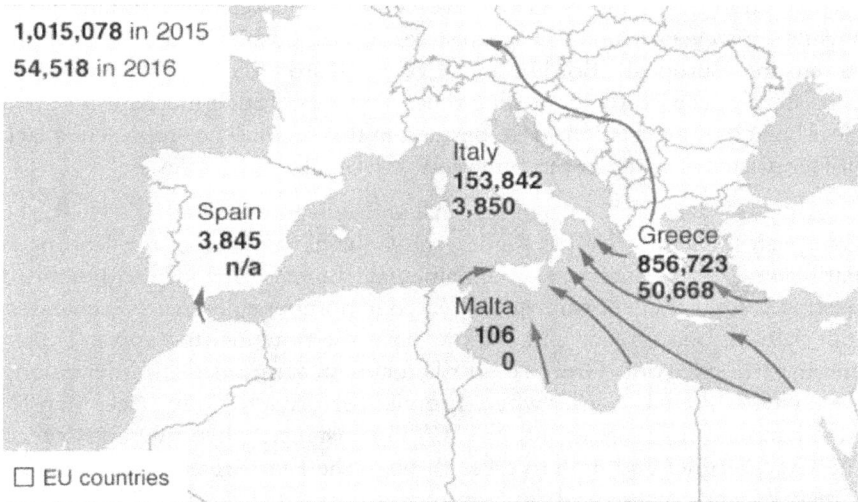

1,015,078 in 2015
54,518 in 2016

Spain
3,845
n/a

Italy
153,842
3,850

Greece
856,723
50,668

Malta
106
0

☐ EU countries

Source: UNHCR

NATO's decision to involve in the refugee crisis came long after the crisis struck the region and the scope of the involvement was not enough to relieve refugees and hosting countries. NATO declared that her task is not to turn boats back, rather it is to provide critical information to Greek and Turkish coastguards, as well as Frontex, to do their job precisely.[28] According to this decision, people who came from Turkey would be taken back to this country. NATO vessels arrived in the Agean Sea within two days and began to conduct their reconnaissance, monitoring, and surveillance activities. Under the Standing NATO Maritime Group II (SNMG2) more than half of a dozen vessels carried out their duties both in territorial waters of the two countries and international waters. Moreover, NATO transformed her counter-terrorism Operation Active Endeavor into a maritime security mission under

---

[26] "Turkey: UNHCR Operational Update January-June 2016", the UNHCR, p. 1.
[27] "EU Migration Crisis Update-June 2016", MSF, 17 June 2016 https://www.msf.org/eu-migration-crisis-update-june-2016 (Access 10.10.2020).
[28] "Statement by the NATO Secretary-General on NATO support to assist with the refugee and migrant crisis", NATO, 25 February 2016, Press Release 024 https://www.nato.int/cps/en/natohq/opinions_128372.htm (Access 11.10.2020).

the name of the Operation Sea Guardian with a broader mandate.[29]

NATO's function in the Mediterranean not only assisted the endeavor of South-Eastern members in their engagement with migrants but also contributed to the cooperation among two maritime rivals of the region. The pressure of millions of migrants over both Turkish society and authorities, the Greek coastguards' inhumane engagement with migrant boats[30] together with the Frontex activities on the land border caused tense relations among the two countries. Thus, NATO's involvement functioned as a facilitator for a while. However, several European states applied pushbacks as a mechanism to ensure European Border and Coast Guard Agency (Frontex) and consistently accused of supporting these activities.[31] Such mechanisms are a clear breach of international law, besides, in this region, they represent a lack of inconsistency in the implementation of EU values and rules.[32]

Although almost all related regional and universal bodies (UNHCR, the European Court of Human Rights, the Council of Europe, the European Parliament, the European Fundamental Rights Agency) condemned pushback cases that enormously increased in number since 2015. Such cases, especially among Greece and Turkey, have the potential to expose Turkey and the EU since only Greece is an EU member. It means the border among two states is the EU border where Frontex performs her duty. (see: Map II-Member states of the EU and NATO) For instance, when migrants forced the Greek border and tried to cross through the Evros river in March 2020, Greek border forces used live ammunition and killed several of them.[33] NATO as a platform where both countries are members came to the stage once more after Turkey pressured both NATO and the EU for their insufficient role and support in the refugee crisis. After EU members accuse Turkey of unleashing migrants to the EU borders NATO Secretary-General warned Europe that it must find a way to work with Turkey:

> "We have to understand that when you speak about the migrant and refugee crisis we speak about a common challenge, which we have to address together... The only way to address the situation on the border is by working together... Turkey is an important ally because Turkey has been key not least in the fight against terrorism, through the global

---

[29] "Operation Sea Guardian", 28 March 2020 https://www.nato.int/cps/en/natohq/topics_136233.htm (Access 01.10.2020).
[30] "Is the Greek coast guard pushing back migrant boats?", DW News https://www.dw.com/en/is-the-greek-coast-guard-pushing-back-migrant-boats/av-54117583 (Access 02.10.2020).
[31] The Council of Europe, "Pushback policies and practice in Council of Europe member States", Parliamentary Assembly Resolution 2299, 2019.
[32] Refugee Rights Europe, "Pushbacks and Rights Violations at European Borders", Position Paper, 2020.
[33] Amnesty International, "Greece/Turkey: Asylum-seekers and migrants killed and abused at borders", 3 April 2020.

coalition to defeat ISIS, NATO allies and NATO have been able to liberate all that territory and all these people, not least by using infrastructure based in Turkey."[34]

Ulgen evaluates threat perceptions of NATO and states that terrorism and the destabilizing impact of refugees came just after Russia as the main source of threat. According to him, there are only two regions concerning NATO with the risk of inter-state war depending on the historical animosities; one is among Greece and Turkey, and the other is among Russia and Finland-Baltic States-Poland.[35] Thus, dealing with the pressure of migrants on the former case is crucial for the future projections of the Alliance.

Map II. Member states of the EU and NATO[36]

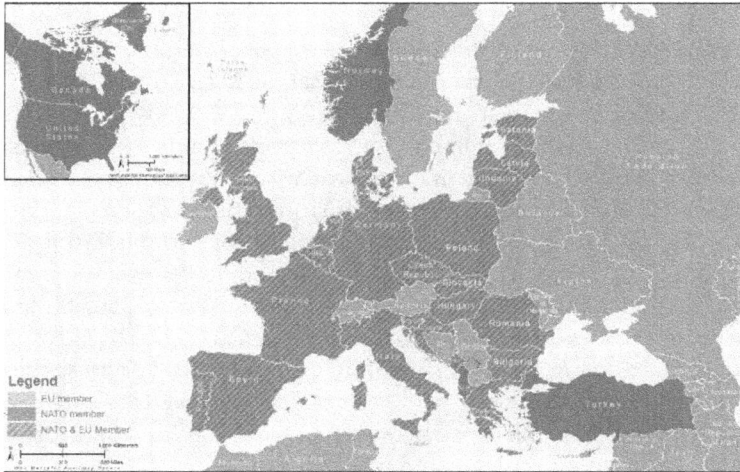

Source: NATO, "Strengthening EU-NATO Relations", 16 July 2019.

In my analysis of NATO's involvement in the refugee crisis, I detected three mechanisms through which NATO might deal with the issue: Civil Emergency Planning Committee (CEPC), Euro-Atlantic Disaster Response Coordination Center (EADRCC), and Civil Emergency Planning Rapid Reaction Team.

CEPC has a long history since the 1950s. It is the top advisory body for the protection of civilians. NATO defines the responsibility area of this committee as humanitarian and disaster response and the protection of

---

[34] Euractiv, "Work with Turkey: NATO tells EU amid migrant crisis", 5 March 2020.
[35] Sinan Ulgen, "A Long-Term Perspective on NATO and the Multinational Order", **Istituto Affari Internazionali**, December 2019, pp. 7-8.
[36] Recently Montenegro joined NATO in June 2017 and North Macedonia in March 2020.

critical infrastructure.[37] Thus, along with the support to the military operations of NATO, supporting the national authorities in cases of civil emergency has been organized within this committee of NATO. By this means, NATO can cooperate with other ministries, rather than the foreign and defense ministries, of the member countries and countries where NATO has operations. Civil Emergency Planning Rapid Reaction Team works to evaluate the needs and capabilities to support a NATO operation or an emergency.[38] In addition to this, a Euro-Atlantic Disaster Response Coordination Center organizes necessary coordination among NATO and other international organizations, such as the UN. While there are many examples of this center's response to emergencies such as the floods in Western Ukraine[39] in June 2020 and the outbreak of the Covid-19 virus pandemic[40], neither the center nor the CEPC did not take necessary actions towards the refugee crisis of the last decade.

However, NATO's existence in Afghanistan, became one of the longest missions in the Alliance history, indicated that such an attitude is possible also in the refugee crisis. For almost 20 years NATO missions provided security in the country, trained local troops, and contributed to reconstruction and development. According to Priyali Sur, NATO's International Security Assistance Force (ISAF) consisted of almost 130.000 troops at its height from 50 countries till the end of the mission in 2014. Resolute Support Mission (RSM), since that time, provided training, assistance, and advice to Afghan security forces.41 Almost 350.000 strong Afghan security forces were built and trained by NATO.42 NATO's future projections may result in focusing on rebuilding broken states and stabilizing conflict areas. The Alliance's experience in Kosovo and Iraq might be a model for peacekeeping and capacity building missions. Only such a mission may reduce the influx of refugees and migrants.

Afghanistan, compared to the sources of instability in the case of the refugee crisis, is far away from NATO borders. Libya, on the other hand, is almost 250-300 km far from the allies' territory while Turkey has a 911 km land border, which is also NATO border, with Syria. These land and sea borders continue to be a hub for human trafficking and smuggling, directly affecting the security of the border country and indirectly affecting the

[37] NATO, "Civil Emergency Planning Committee",
https://www.nato.int/cps/en/natohq/topics_50093.htm (Access 12.10.2020).
[38] Judy Dempsey, op. cit.
[39] NATO, "Floods in Ukraine" EADRCC Situation Report No 2, 10 August 2020, p. 2.
[40] NATO, "NATO Response to Covid-19", 04 October 2020 https://www.nato.int/cps/en/natohq/news_174271.htm (Access 12.10.2020).
[41] Priyali Sur, "A strong NATO could help alleviate the world's migrant and refugee crisis", 24 April 2019, Atlantic Council, p. 2.
[42] NATO, "NATO and Europe's refugee and migrant crisis", 26 February 2016 https://www.nato.int/cps/en/natohq/opinions_128645.htm (Access 14.10.2020).

security of the Alliance. Once more diverging interests of Russia and the USA in addition to the regional powers Turkey, Iran, Egypt, and Israel are leaving NATO allies with a little military margin of maneuver.[43] Despite the Allies' divergence of interests NATO has already conducted activities in the southern neighborhood to project stability in the region:

a. Defense and security capacity building in Iraq,

b. The Resolute Support Mission in Afghanistan,

c. Supporting Tunisia in her counter-terrorism fight through pilot projects,

d. The Sea Guardian Operation in the Mediterranean,

e. The establishment of a hub for the South in Joint Force Command Naples,

f. The Allied Ground Surveillance System (AGS) based on the Italian base of Sigonella,

g. The establishment of an Assistant Secretary-General for Intelligence in 2016.

Although it seems all these are not enough to counter security threats in the region, Bianchi and others assert that NATO is not and should not be a first responder since there is no fix solution:

"At first glance, NATO seems to do a lot, but in a fractured and not very inclusive way. One of the main reasons is that with respect to security challenges in the southern neighbourhood, such as terrorism, instability, conflicts, and the related migratory crisis affecting Europe, NATO is not and should not be a first responder. National authorities, the EU, and ad hoc coalitions including many Allies have been at the forefront. To mention two examples: the EU has launched the aforementioned mission Sophia, while Italy has run the two maritime operations Mare Nostrum and then Mare Sicuro and has actively supported the Libyan government recognized by the international community. Indeed, NATO's role to project stability in the southern neighbourhood should be framed largely in terms of cooperation, support and synergy with other actors, including Alliance members and partners. This adds a further layer of complexity, but it is the only way

[43] Rod Thornton, "Countering Prompt Global Strike: The Russian Military Presence in Syria and the Eastern Mediterranean and Its Strategic Deterrence Role", **The Journal of Slavic Military Studies,** Vol. 32, No. 1, pp. 1-24.

to make progress in the region since there is no quick fix solution for the security challenges in that area."[44]

Bianchi's point clarifies the situation within which NATO is stuck. Converging approaches of the member states leave the Alliance inactive. Moreover, as in the case of disagreement among Greece and Turkey over the Eastern Mediterranean recently, fractures within NATO makes it complicated to reach a prudent decision.

From Ensuring State Security to the Security of People

The role that they cast for NATO is not an Alliance intervening in the conflict region and halting the civil war. Since members of the Alliance are not like-minded almost in all conflict areas of the MENA, the role of NATO is to assist member or neighbor countries to prevent escalation. Some experts define this process as enriching NATO's toolbox by bringing soft power[45] to its repertoire.[46] NATO has already stated that law enforcement activities will take place within the future operations.[47] Although NATO as a military collective defense organization focuses on conventional defense and deterrence, her role in civil crisis might be overlooked especially after the covid-19 pandemic outbreak. The EADRCC, despite strong criticism about her insufficient actions in the refugee crisis, played a very important role in response to the covid-19 pandemic. The center was active in West Africa in combat against Ebola, in Bulgaria and Ukraine to combat the H1N1, and most recently it helped deliver ventilators and masks from Turkey, Germany, and the Czech Republic to Italy and Spain.[48] This should be seen as a test case since Turkey, despite all geopolitical tensions, came to help the members of the Alliance and displayed a spirit of union for the future of NATO.

In addition to the role of NATO in the pandemics, the Alliance has experience in wide-ranging areas from earthquakes, forest fires, floods to chemical attacks. The 2018 chemical attacks in the UK were a clear reflection of the need for such an infrastructure and preparedness. The humanitarian assistance to the refugees of the Kosovo War glorified NATO's role as ensuring the security of the people in addition to the state security. However, refugees in huge numbers during the last decade damaged her prestige as an Alliance ensuring the security of the people. In my opinion, the experience that NATO gained from the civil crisis is crucial for her future operations.

---

[44] Bianchi, op. cit., p. 8.
[45] For further information about the concept, please see: Joseph S. Nye, Soft Power: The Means To Success In World Politics, Public Affairs, 2005.
[46] Sarantaki, op. cit., p. 15.
[47] NATO, "The Future Security Environment: Challenges and Opportunities", Chapter I, Framework for Future Alliance Operations Report, 2018, pp. 13-20.
[48] Lauren Speranza, "Six reasons NATO's Euro-Atlantic Disaster Response Coordination Centre is important for our future security", The Atlantic, 7 April 2020.

Security threats of this century seem to come not only from the military. Climate change may displace people in huge numbers and NATO should have prepared and experienced to respond it until this time. That is why today's refugee crisis is an opportunity for NATO to respond and improve her capacity to pursue the security of the people alongside state security. That is why the Alliance has to overcome fractures in case of the refugee crisis not only to ameliorate the lives of these people but also to present an alliance capable to do it.

Conclusion

This study tried to analyze NATO's position towards the current refugee crisis. The scope of the crisis was dealt with to clarify the issue and to present why it should be one of the Alliance's duties. This paper also sheds light on the Alliance's long history in her policies towards the refugees. It became clear that NATO has to overcome the destabilizer effect of this crisis both to help to ameliorate the lives of these people and to solve potential fractures within the alliance.

Since it became clear that NATO has the capacity to perform this duty when her response to other humanitarian crises is analyzed, the focus became internal fractures. NATO's inability to act against this crisis depends on the converging interests of the members. Moreover, the issue is not only the willingness or unwillingness of the members to welcome refugees, but it is the members' diverging approaches towards the source country. Turkey's feelings of being left alone by both the EU and NATO, disagreement among the EU, Greece and Turkey over border policies, and conflicting foreign policy preferences towards Syria, Libya, and other unstable countries tied NATO's hands in solving the crisis.

Nevertheless, it is necessary to state two significant points related to NATO's position on the refugee crisis. The first one is the possibility that while NATO focuses on the security of the people rather than state security, diverging interests and foreign policy preferences of the members might cause problems weakening actual operational abilities. Thus, it may indirectly damage state security despite NATO has been a collective security organization since the beginning. The second one is the possibility that while NATO tries to prioritize the security of the people, it may cause the militarization of the policies towards the refugees as in the case of harsh critics of the Frontex activities. Further research on these two points seems to be a good contribution to this area of study.

CHAPTER 7

REFUGEE POLICIES OF COUNCIL OF EUROPE

Furkan Yıldız[*]

Introduction

While, in international law, the refugee occupies a legal area implied by the principle of state sovereignty and the related principles of superiority and self-protection; on the other hand, it competes with humanitarian principles of general international law.[1] Apart from legal dimension, refugee issue has a humanitarian aspect. According to the numbers of the United Nations High Commissioner for Refugees, there are 79.5 million people worldwide forcibly displaced at the end of 2019. Almost 33% (26 million) of total number of forcibly displaced people is refugees and 5.25% (4.2 million) of the total number is asylum-seekers.[2] In this regard, the humanitarian dimension of the issue is as important as its legal and political dimensions.

With the Geneva Convention, which was accepted by the United Nations in 1951 and became the leading instrument of international law, the definitions and rights of refugees were set forth.[3] According to the Article 1A(2) of the Convention, a refugee as "*a person who is outside his or her country of nationality or habitual residence; has a well-founded fear of being persecuted because of his or her race, religion, nationality, membership of a particular social group or political opinion; and is unable or unwilling to avail him or herself of the protection of that country, or to return there, for fear of persecution.*"[4] After this significant step of international community, the concept of refugee and refugee rights has become an area where international organizations such as the European Union and Council of Europe and regional organizations such as the Asia Pacific Refugee Rights Network Visions for Regional Protection and Association of Southeast Asian Nations (ASEAN) take actions. The Council of Europe, which is one of these organizations that draws attention both with its number of members and with its establishment goals, will be the focus of this study. The Council of Europe

[*] Assistant Professor Kirklareli University, Vocational School Of Social Sciences, Head of Foreign Trade Department
[1] Guy S. Goodwin-Gill and Jane McAdam, **The Refugee in International Law**, New York, Oxford University Press, 2007, p.1.
[2] UNHCR, "Figures at Glance", https://www.unhcr.org/figures-at-a-glance.html (Access 11.10.2020).
[3] Nuala Mole, **Asylum and The European Convention on Human Rights**, Strasburg, Council of Europe Publishing, 2003, p. 6.
[4] UNHCR, "The 1951 Convention Relating to the Status of Refugees and Its 1967 Protocol" https://www.unhcr.org/about-us/background/4ec262df9/1951-convention-relating-status-refugees-its-1967-protocol.html (Access 22.06.2020), p.3.

was established in 1949. Its main objectives are to protect human rights, the rule of law, democracy, standardize the development of states in the European continent, and protect the values that form the basis of Europe while respecting the values of different cultures.[5] The Council of Europe, which currently has 47 members, has all its actions structured around these values. The Council of Europe, which focuses on the protection of human rights, aims to achieve this goal by taking action in four areas. These are effective supervision and protection of fundamental rights and freedoms; identifying new threats to human rights and human dignity; developing public awareness of the importance of human rights; promoting human rights education and professional training.[6]

As an intergovernmental institution, the Council of Europe supports its members by working in many different fields. One of these areas is Special Representative on Migration and Refugees appointed by the Secretary General of the Council of Europe. Under his mandate, the Special Representative provides advice to the Secretary-General and member States on the legal aspects of human rights standards relating to migration stemming from the European Convention on Human Rights and other relevant Council of Europe documents. These recommendations include how to strengthen human rights practices for refugees and migrants and how to improve practices for these groups in Europe.[7]

In this context, the steps taken by the Council of Europe regarding refugees will be examined and examples will be given by drawing a general framework. In this direction, the norms of the European Convention on Human Rights (ECHR) will be investigated.

Practices Related to Refugees in the Council of Europe and the European Convention on Human Rights

The European Convention on Human Rights (ECHR), adopted in Rome in 1950 and made within the framework of the Council of Europe, undertakes to comply with the civil and political rights and freedoms of the parties. In addition to the ECHR, the members of the Council of Europe are also obliged to fulfil the requirements of the 1951 Geneva Convention.[8] This

---

[5] "Council of Europe", https://www.refworld.org/publisher/COE.html (Access 11.10.2020).
[6] "The Council of Europe and language policy for migrants/refugees",https://www.coe.int/tr/web/language-support-for-adult-refugees/the-council-of-europe-and-language-policy-for-migrants/refugees (Access 11.09.2020).
[7] "Legal work", https://www.coe.int/en/web/special-representative-secretary-general-migration-refugees/legal-work (Access 15.09.2020).
[8] The United Nations Convention on the Status of Refugees, adopted in 1951, based on Article 14 of the Universal Declaration of Human Rights of 1948, which recognizes the right to seek asylum in order to escape persecution in other countries, is the most important element of the international refugee protection system today. The Convention entered into force on April 22, 1954 and was amended only once by the 1967 New York Protocol to the Geneva Convention, Article 1(2), which abolished the

could be the most significant step of the Council related to refugees without using particular instruments on refugees.[9] The Convention embodied the 1948 Universal Declaration of Human Rights and established an international court that could convict states that did not fulfil their obligations. Due to the jurisprudence and comments put forward by this court, the provisions of the Convention have become a living and continuously developing instrument of international law.[10]

Before moving on to the articles of the ECHR related to refugees, it is useful to look at the differences between the practices of the ECHR and the Geneva Convention. The most important difference between the two documents is that ECHR does not have any articles directly related to refugees. Other differences are made through the definition of refugees made by the Geneva Convention. First, the scope of application of ECHR is wider in terms of subject and person, because while the 1951 Geneva Convention seeks certain conditions while defining the persons who will benefit from the Convention, everyone in the states that are parties to the ECHR can benefit from the rights protected by the ECHR.[11] While in the 1951 Geneva Convention, a person must be outside his/her country to apply for refugee status, there are no restrictions in this regard in the ECHR. Contrary to the conditions of the Geneva Convention related to fear relevant to persons' race, religion and nationality, the ECHR provides protection to a person to be subjected to inhumane treatment regardless of the cause of the fear.[12] In the 1951 Geneva Convention, the condition of not being able to benefit from the state protection sought to benefit from the refugee status does not exist in the ECHR.[13] Beside these differences, those who will benefit from refoulement have not been regulated in the ECHR, but the situations (...*reasonable grounds for regarding as a danger to the security of the country in which he is, or who, having been convicted by a final judgment of a particularly serious crime, constitutes a danger to the community of that country*) to benefit from refoulement are listed in Article 33(2) of the Geneva Convention. As can be seen, there

---

geographical and temporal boundaries of the 1951 Convention.

[9] In the European Convention on Human Rights (ECHR), although there is no direct regulation regarding refugees and asylum seekers, the relevant articles (arts. 3/8/13/34) in the context of protecting human rights can also be applied to protect the rights of refugees and asylum seekers. Neslihan Özkerim Güner, "Avrupa İnsan Hakları Mahkemesi'nin Mültecilerin Haklarının Korunmasındaki Rolü", **Göç Araştırmaları Dergisi**, Vol. 2, No. 2, 2016, p. 214

[10] Osman Doğru and Atilla Nalbant, **İnsan Hakları Avrupa Sözleşmesi**, Vol 1, İstanbul, Legal Yayıncılık, 2012, p.2-4.

[11] Güner, op.cit., p.214.

[12] Jane McAdam, **Complementary Protection in International Refugee Law**, New York, Oxford University Press, 2007, p.21: Harald Dörig, "Judicial experience with the Geneva Convention in Germany and Europe", **The UNHCR and the Supervision of International Refugee Law**, James C. Simeon (Ed.), Cambridge, Cambridge University Press, 2013, p.150: Mole, op.cit., p.10.

[13] Vanessa Bettinson, "Loss and Denial of Refugee Status", **An Introduction to International Refugee Law**, Rafiqul Islam and Jahid Hossain Bhuiyan (Eds.), Leiden, Martinus Nijhoff Publishers, 2013, p.87: McAdam, op.cit, p.198: Güner, op.cit. p.215:

are differences in implementation between the two Conventions. In this context, it can be said that the ECHR has a wider application area than the 1951 Geneva Convention.

Regulations of the ECHR and their Applications into Refugees Related Cases in European Court of Human Rights (ECtHR)

As mentioned earlier, the ECHR has neither made a direct regulation of the refugees' situation nor addressed the rights related to asylum. Nevertheless, there are several regulations that could be used in refugee and asylum relevant situations. These are "prohibition of torture"[14], "right to liberty and security"[15], "right to respect for private and family life"[16], and "right to an effective remedy."[17] Apart from the practices related to these regulations, this section examines decisions and recommendations of the Council of Europe's Committee of Ministers and Parliamentary Assembly.

ECtHR and the Application of Art. 3 in the Case Laws

With regard to the prohibition of torture, inhuman or degrading treatment or punishment (Art.3), the ECHR has interpreted to include *non-refoulement* component.[18] In other word, violation of Article 3 is generally alleged in case of violation of the principle of *non-refoulement*.[19] This principle means that a person whose fundamental rights and freedoms are endangered due to their race, religion, nationality, social group or political view should not be returned to the country of origin.[20] Although this principle is regulated in Article 33 of the Geneva Convention, it now covers all foreigners, as this principle has become the rule of international customary law.[21] Article 33 prohibits two situations: "expel" which means to prohibit sending a person not only to the country of origin, but also to a third country where they may be in danger and "return" which means he prohibition on returning the person to a country where their freedom is in danger is prohibited.[22] About removal to a third country, in *Ilias and Ahmed v. Hungary*[23], ECtHR observed

---

[14] Art. 3 of ECHR
[15] Art. 5 of ECHR
[16] Art. 8 of ECHR
[17] Art. 13 of ECHR
[18] Lilian Tsourdi, "Regional Regimes: Europe", **Oxford Handbook for International Refugee Law**, Cathryn Costello, Michelle Foster and Jane McAdam (Eds.), New York, Oxford University Press, (Forthcoming), p.9.
[19] Directorate General of Human Rights and Legal Affairs, **Human Rights Protection in the Context of Accelerated Asylum Procedures (H/INF (2009) 4**, Strasburg, Council of Europe, 2009, p.37.
[20] Hélène Lambert, The position of aliens in relation to the European Convention on Human Rights, Strasburg, Council of Europe Publishing, p.48.
[21] Jean Allain,"The Jus Cogens Nature on Non-refoulent", **International Journal of Refugee Law**, Vol.13, No.4, 2002, p537: Nuray Ekşi, **Yabancılar ve Koruma Hukuku**, İstanbul, Beta, 2014, p.63.
[22] Güner, op.cit. p.218.
[23] By agreement between the European Community and the Republic of Serbia on the readmission of

that where a Contracting State attempted to send the asylum seeker to a third country without adequate or no examination of the merits of the asylum claim, the State's duty of not exposing the individual to the risk of treatment contrary to Article 3 was somewhat fulfilled.[24] It is the occurrence of various problems even if there is observation and control. For instance, it may be occurred that inadequate admission requirements of the receiving state[25] or their access to safe reception facilities[26] are not guaranteed. In this point, the removing State shall receive assurances from the receiving State regarding the performance of the said matters. In this regard, Parliamentary Assembly Recommendation 1327 (1997) recommended that the member states should not apply the principles of "safe third country" and "safe country of origin" in an arbitrary manner.[27] According to the Recommendation, the member states should set precise criteria in relation to the "safe" country concept, in line with the recommendations of the Ad hoc Committee of Experts on the Legal Aspects of Territorial Asylum, Refugees and Stateless Persons (CAHAR).

Soering v United Kingdom (1989) underlined that individuals could be sent to States where the ECHR measures were not fully met.[28] According to Article 3, which prohibits inhumane practices such as torture and degrading treatment, individuals cannot be sent to countries where they face real risks of being exposed to such treatment.[29] If there is a risk in the receiving country regarding matters covered by Article 6 of the ECHR (right to a fair trial) in relation to a person, the return may be prohibited as an exception.[30] In this case, ECtHR found a violation of Article 3 of the ECHR and accepted the application. In other words, the Court's precedent decision is that an individual cannot be sent to a country where there is a risk of torture, inhuman treatment or punishment.[31]

One of the important decisions in which Article 3 was applied was taken in the case of *Jabari v. Turkey.*[32] The applicant is an Iranian national and was detained in Iran in October 1997 after being publicly arrested with a married man. She was released with the help of family and illegally enters in Turkey

---

persons residing without authorisation, removal to a third country regime has been implemented. This agreement, approved by Council Decision 2007/819/EC of 8 November 2007.

[24] *Ilias and Ahmed v. Hungary* (2019) (Application no. 47287/15),para 59.

[25] *Tarakhel v. Switzerland* (2014) (Application no. 29217/12), para 10.

[26] *Ali and Others v. Switzerland and Italy* (2016) (Application no. 30474/14), para 4.

[27] Parliamentary Assembly Recommendation 1327 (1997) on Protection and reinforcement of the human rights of refugees and asylum-seekers in Europe, para. 8.7(d).

[28] *Soering v United Kingdom* (1989) 11 EHRR 439, para 86.

[29] *Saadi v Italy* (2008) 47 EHRR 17

[30] *Othman (Abu Qatada) v United Kingdom* (2012) 55 EHRR 1: Soering, op.cit., para 113.

[31] Soering, op.cit. para 91: Sibel Yılmaz, "Protection of Refugees' Rights Arising out of The International Protection Procedure from the View of Turkish Constitutional Court's Individual Application Decisions", **Ankara Üni. Hukuk Fak. Dergisi**, Vol. 68, No. 3, 2019, p.714.

[32] Jabari v.Turkey (2000), (Application no. 40035/98), Decision 11.10.2000.

in November 1997. Later, she took action by using a fake passport to go to Canada, and during this time she was caught and detained in France. She was returned to Istanbul, where she was arrested for entering on a forged passport. During this period, the applicant, who sought asylum, was refused on two grounds. First, she was rejected because of the application had been submitted out of time. Second, the applicant should have registered within 5 days of her arrival in compliance with the Asylum Regulation 1994 but she has not registered. On 16 February 1998 the applicant was recognized as a refugee by the UNHCR in order to protect her from the severe and inhumane punishments she might face if sent to Iran.[33] The significance of the case is the Court's decision increased the envisaged 5-day registration period to 10 days.[34] In *Ghorbanov and others v Turkey* case, the ECtHR decided that there has been a violation of Article 3. The arbitrary return of 19 Uzbek refugees to Iran was considered inhumane treatment and the deportation decision did not establish procedural safeguards.[35]

In the case of *Rahimi v. Greece*, the Court justified the application of the defendant, who received accommodation and care services by NGOs, while the requirements of Article 3 of the ECHR had to be met by the relevant state. With such a determination, the Court transformed a civil right, which should be respected regardless of the available resources, into a social right requiring substantial expenditure.[36] In addition, such a decision to that effect forced the government to spend on refugees' rights and to meet other legal demands.[37]

ECtHR and the Application of Art. 5 in the Case Laws

In this article, Convention regulated the "right to liberty and security". Article 5 (1) f, which is "the lawful arrest or detention of a person to prevent his effecting an unauthorised entry into the country or of a person against whom action is being taken with a view to deportation or extradition", can be applied only aliens. Under this subheading, two case law from ECtHR

---

[33] EDAL, "Jabari v. Turkey, Application no. 40035/98, 11 July 2000-Case Summary", https://www.asylumlawdatabase.eu/en/content/ecthr-jabari-v-turkey-application-no-4003598-11-july-2000 (Access 10.10.2020).

[34] Levent Korkut, "Avrupa İnsan Hakları Mahkemesi Kararlarının Devletlerin Sığınmacıları Sınır Dışı Etme Egemen Yetkisine Etkisi: Türkiye Örneği", **Ankara Barosu Dergisi**, Vol. 66, No.4, 2008, p.28: Güner, op.cit., p.223. In 2006, ten days restriction was removed. It has been added to the 1994 Regulation that the application for asylum must be made without any delay. This regulation was repealed in 2014 by Temporary Protection Regulation.

[35] Ghorbanov and others v Turkey (2013) (Application No. 28127/09), para 32.

[36] Marc Bossuyt, "Belgium Condemned for Inhuman or Degrading Treatment Due to Violations by Greece of EU Asylum Law: MSS v. Belgium and Greece", **European Human Rights Law Review**, 2011, pp.591-593.

[37] Marc Bossuyt,, "Is the European Court of Human Rights on a slippery slope?", **The European Court of Human Rights and its Discontents: Turning Criticism into Strength**, Spyridon Flogaitis, Tom Zwart and Julie Fraser (Eds.), Cheltenham, Edward Elgar, 2013, p.32.

related to application of the Article 5(1)f has been assessed. In the case of Riad and Idiab v. Belgium, Palestinian refugees were detained at the airport on the grounds that they did not have valid travel documents to enter the country, and were deprived of their basic needs by not being allowed to leave despite the absence of a lawful detention order for days.[38] The Court made a decision against Belgium's attitude expressed as deprivation of liberty because of the violation of Art.5 (unlawful detention)[39] and Art. 3 (long and without basic needs).

In the case of *Musaev v. Turkey,* The Uzbek national applicant was detained as part of a murder investigation before he sought asylum. He was cleared of the murder investigation because he had witness statements in his favor, but continued to be detained. Moreover, he was transferred to Kumkapı Removal Centre for deportation. During this period, the applicant, who applied for asylum, received a temporary residence permit pending the consideration of his application to the United Nations High Commissioner for Refugees and the Ministry of Interior.[40] During this period, the applicant was detained for twenty-seven days without any explanation regarding the legal basis of his detention and the reasons for his detention. Moreover, he was not given a right of appeal or any compensation during this period. In other words, he does not have access to domestic legal mechanisms. The ECtHR has held Turkey to be in violation of the applicant's right to liberty and to exceed the material reception conditions during his detention. Furthermore, the Court found that the applicant had been deprived of an effective remedy to make any complaint and appeal.[41]

Regarding to this point, governments should establish a system that improves the quality of the decision making processes. Increased quality in decision making processes makes all relevant processes fairer, more effective and faster.[42] In addition to the steps of policy makers related to processes, the competence of their staff, especially those involved in first responders, is important for ensuring liberty and security. In particular with regard to

---

[38] *Riad and Idiab v. Belgium* (2008) (Applications nos. 29787/03 and 29810/03), para. 26-43.

[39] *MSS and Rahimi Groups v. Greece,* (App no 30696/09), 1348th meeting, 4-6 June 2019 (DH), As a decision, Committee of Ministers recommends to Greece on the degrading treatment of the applicants (asylum seekers or irregular migrants, including unaccompanied minors) on account of their conditions of detention, para. 1.

[40] EDAL "Musaev v. Turkey (Application No. 72754/11), 21 October 2014-Case Summary" https://www.asylumlawdatabase.eu/en/content/ecthr-%E2%80%93-musaev-v-turkey-application-no-7275411 (Access 22.09.2020).

[41] These kind of unlawful exercises are also against the rules of the Turkish Constitution provide as follows: Art.36 of the Constitution underlines the importance of fair trial as "Everyone has the right to a fair trial ..., as a claimant or defendant, before courts of law ...". Art. 125 of the Constitution declares "All actions or decision taken by the authorities are amenable to judicial review". In these respect, the case was not only about just the international human rights law but also about the domestic procedural mechanisms.

[42] Directorate General of Human Rights and Legal Affairs, op.cit. p.41.

detention, Recommendation 1309 (1996) of the Parliamentary Assembly underlines that *"the officials' knowledge and skills should be developed by the limitations under national and international law on the use of detention, and the guidelines of the Office of the United Nations High Commissioner for Refugees (UNHCR) on this subject."* [43] In these aforementioned points, the Council of Europe and ECtHR drew the rules to be obeyed by the officials and governments regarding the non-restriction of liberty and the security of the refugees within the framework of human rights and took decisions to prevent any violation in practice.

ECtHR and the Application of Art. 8 in the Case Laws

This article protects the right to respect for family life, separation of families does not alone give rise to a right for family members to enter and reunite in a state.[44] In this respect, in the event of deportation, it should be checked whether the family is likely to be reunited in another country. Also, if a third country accepts a refugee, it must also grant admission to other family members in order to maintain family unity.[45] The case law has evolved over time to make human rights more protective, especially when it comes to children's rights.

The ECtHR has been sensitive to the particular situation of refugees and has strengthened the practices regarding the protection of family reunification rights. In the case of *Tuquabo-Tekle v. the Netherlands,* a mother left her daughter behind when she fled to seek refuge in Eritrea after her husband's death. The Court doubted whether the mother had left her daughter behind "her own free will". Because of this suspicion, the Court decided that the Netherlands was obliged to admit the woman's daughter to the country in accordance with Article 8 of the Convention so that they could enjoy family life in the country together.[46] In the light of this decision, it is true to say that family reunification is often the only way to protect refugees' right to respect for family life with their current protection needs. As a matter of fact, this approach was demonstrated both in *Tanda-Muzinga v. France*[47] and *Mugenzi v. France*[48] cases in 2014. Both applicants are individuals with refugee status in France who applied for family reunification in 2003 and 2007 respectively, and in both cases the children are in the third country. Both have encountered difficulties associated with the procedure.[49] In the *Mugenzi* case,

---

[43] Recommendation 1309 (1996), Doc. 7683, report of the Committee on Migration, Refugees and Demography, rapporteur: Mr Akselsen. Text adopted by the Standing Committee, acting on behalf of the Assembly, on 7 November 1996.
[44] McAdam, op.cit.p.16.
[45] Terje Einarsen, "The European Convention on Human Rights and the Notion of an Implied Right to de facto Asylum" **International Journal of Refugee Law**, Vol. 2, No. 3, 1990, p.375.
[46] *Tuquabo-Tekle v. the Netherlands* (2004) (Application no. 60665/00).
[47] *Tanda-Muzinga v. France* (2014) (Application no. 2260/10).
[48] *Mugenzi v. France* (2014) (Application no. 52701/09).
[49] Council of Europe Commissioner for Human Rights, "Realising the right to family reunification of

a cursory dental examination was carried out to cast doubt on the date on the birth certificate, and the application for family reunification was rejected for this reason. In the *Tanda-Muzinga* case, the authorities questioned the authenticity of the identity documents in order not to grant the right to family reunification. However, after several years of appeals and difficulties, the applicant gained the right to family reunification. In the *Mugenzi* case, the mechanisms to appeal the court's findings on dental records became dysfunctional, and the children became adults in the process.

In addition to family reunification, Article 8 emphasizes another significant issue. During detention process, asylum seekers should not held together with ordinary prisoners and men and women should be accommodated separately. There is one exception to this situation. In accordance with the principle of privacy of individuals' private and family lives, and principle of the unity of the family, family members should therefore be accommodated accordingly.[50]

ECtHR and the Application of Art. 13

"Right to an effective remedy" is regulated under Art.13 which provides a certain degree of protection for refugees in cases relevant to extradition, deportation and return.[51] In this article, right to an effective remedy is described, as: "*Everyone whose rights and freedoms as set forth in this Convention are violated shall have an effective remedy before a national authority notwithstanding that the violation has been committed by persons acting in an official capacity.*" In this respect, the right to an effective remedy is important in order to prevent loss of any rights.[52] In addition to Article 13 of ECHR, Recommendation R (98) 13 of the Committee of Ministers[53] has also proclaimed on the right of rejected asylum seekers to an effective remedy against decisions on expulsion in the context of Article 3 of the European Convention. Even if they have not underlined about an effective remedy openly, Parliamentary Assembly Recommendation 1327 (1997)[54] and Parliamentary Assembly Recommendation 1236 (1994)[55] also highlighted that the rights of refugees in judicial processes. On 19 September 2001, the Council of Europe

refugees in Europe", https://rm.coe.int/prems-052917-gbr-1700-realising-refugees-160x240-web/1680724ba0 (Access 22.06.2020).

[50] Directorate General of Human Rights and Legal Affairs, op.cit. p.55.

[51] Bülent Çiçekli, **Yabacılar ve Mülteci Hukuku**, Ankara, Seçkin Yayıncılık, 2014, p.241.

[52] The Art.6 of the Convention emphasizes the right to a fair trial. This means that everyone has the right to a fair and public hearing within a reasonable time by an independent and impartial tribunal established by law. However, refugees cannot benefit from this right, as the asylum and deportation cases are not under civil rights and obligations or in criminal investigations. Einarsen, op.cit. p. 377.

[53] Committee of Ministers, Recommendation N° R (98) 13 on the Right of Rejected Asylum Seekers to an Effective Remedy Against Decisions on Expulsion in the Context of Article 3 of the European Convention on Human Rights, 18 September 1998, para.1.

[54] Parliamentary Assembly Recommendation 1327 (1997), op.cit. para. 8.7.

[55] Parliamentary Assembly Recommendation 1236 (1994) on the right of asylum, para. 8(ii)/d.

Commissioner for Human Rights issued a Recommendation (CommDH (2001) 19) on the rights of foreigners wishing to enter a Council of Europe member state and the implementation of deportation decisions. According to this Recommendation, The right of effective remedy must be guaranteed to anyone wishing to challenge a *refoulement* or expulsion order.[56]

Conclusion

The Council of Europe, an intergovernmental institution, produces binding decisions after the approval of the relevant member states. About migrants and refugees, important actions of the Council of Europe are generally at the political level and include recommendations to the Council of Ministers of the member countries, conventions and resolutions, as well as regular discussions and reports prepared in the Parliamentary Assembly.[57] The Council of Europe influences policies related to refugees through the practice of aforementioned decision-making and non-judicial institutions.[58]

The Council of Europe strives to support refugees in many different areas. For instance, the Council prepares a toolkit for adult refugees to provide language support to them.[59] The Council not only strives for adult refugees, but also prepared an action plan for the problems of children may face. It covers recommendations and policy directives to member states on protecting refugee and migrant children in Europe.[60] After the COVID-19 outbreak occurred, Council of Europe support member states in bringing refugee health workers into fight against pandemic with UNHCR.[61] Striving for the more humane aspects of international law rather than the normative side, the Council of Europe has also prepared a handbook for family reunification protected by the ECHR, setting standards and possible future practices.[62]

The Council of Europe, which takes steps for the legal status of refugees

---

[56] CommDH(2001)19, Recommendation of the Commissioner for Human Rights Concerning the rights of aliens wishing to enter a Council of Europe member State and the enforcement of expulsion orders, para. 11.

[57] https://rm.coe.int/arac-2-multecilerin-haklar-ve-yasal-konumlar-temel-bilgi-ve-terimler-y/1680761f8c (Access 11.09.2020).

[58] Tsourdi, op.cit. p.10.

[59] Council of Europe, "Language support to adult refugees: the Council of Europe toolkit", https://www.coe.int/en/web/language-policy/adult-refugees (Access 01.10.2020).

[60] Council of Europe, "Council of Europe Action Plan on Protecting Refugee and Migrant Children in Europe (2017-2019)", Ref. 081117GBR, https://edoc.coe.int/en/children-s-rights/7362-council-of-europe-action-plan-on-protecting-refugee-and-migrant-children-in-europe-2017-2019.html (Access 11.10.2020).

[61] https://www.coe.int/en/web/portal/-/council-of-europe-and-unhcr-support-member-states-in-bringing-refugee-health-workers-into-the-fight-against-covid-19 (Access 06.06.2020)

[62] Council of Europe, " Family reunification for Refugee and Migrant Children" https://rm.coe.int/family-reunification-for-refugee-and-migrant-children-standards-and-pr/16809e8320 (Access 19.08. 2020).

as well as their social rights, prepared a report for the member states in 2005 to help them speed up their asylum process.[63] In this report, the Parliamentary Assembly invites the governments of the member states of the Council of Europe as regards the general use of accelerated procedure (*non-refoulement*, minimum procedural guarantees equally for all asylum applications etc.), the concept of safe country of origin, the concept of safe third country, including the concept of "super safe third country", border applicants, the duration of the procedure, time limits etc.

As can be seen, the Council of Europe takes steps on many issues related to refugees with an interdisciplinary approach. By combining legal and political approaches with social and humanitarian approaches, it advises member states on all kinds of problems that refugees may encounter. In this context, both the Council and the ECtHR, which is the council's executive tool, seeks solutions for refugees and supports its members.

---

[63] https://assembly.coe.int/nw/xml/XRef/X2H-Xref-ViewHTML.asp?FileID=10980&lang=EN #P462_70727

CHAPTER 8

THE IMPACT OF INTERNATIONAL TRADE ORGANIZATIONS ON THE REFUGEE CRISIS

Hazar Dördüncü*

Introduction

"To reject a struggling migrant, whatever his or her religious belief, out of fear of diluting a 'Christian' culture is grotesquely mispresenting both Christianity and culture."

"Migration is not a threat to Christianity except in the minds of those who benefit from claiming it is".

"To promote the Gospel and not welcome the strangers in need, nor affirm their humanity as children of God, is to seek to encourage a culture that is Christian in name only, emptied of all that makes it distinctive."

The pontiff who is the grandson of Italian emigrants who settled in Argentina made the comments in "Let Us Dream", a new book written in conversation with British biographer Austen Ivereigh.

"The dignity of our peoples demands safe corridors for migrants and refugees so they can move without fear from deadly areas to safer ones," he said in the book.

"It is unacceptable to deter immigration by letting hundreds of migrants die in perilous sea crossings or desert treks. The Lord will ask us to account for each one of those deaths."

"A fantasy of national-populism in countries with Christian majorities is its defence of 'Christian civilization' from perceived enemies, whether Islam, Jews, the European Union or the United Nations," he said.[1]

Despite the statements of Pope, it can be seen from the reports and the statistics provided by the Amnesty International and the United Nations Refugee Agency (UNHCR) that particularly the Christian countries or international trade organizations that are mainly consisted of Christian

* Nişantaşı University, School of Applied Sciences, Department of International Trade and Business Administration, Turkey. E-mail: hazar.dorduncu@nisantasi.edu.tr. ORCID ID: 0000-0002-9481-2063
[1] https://www.euronews.com/2020/11/23/migration-is-not-a-threat-to-christianity-says-pope-francis (Access 23.11.2020).

countries take place at the bottom of the lists on migrant accommodation.[2]

According to the numbers of UNCHR, there are a total number of 26 million refugees in the world; 20.4 million being within UNHCR's knowledge; and 5.6 million of them being the Palestine Refugees in the Near East as indicated by The United Nations Relief and Works Agency (UNRWA). It is also observed that 45.7 million people are forced for displacement, 4.2 million people carry the status of asylum-seekers, and 3.6 million replaced people due to conflict in Venezuela, all together adding up to the fact that 1% of the world's population is forced to migrate.[3]

The 80% of those people who are forced to migrate, migrated due to bad living conditions caused by factors such as acute food insecurity and malnutrition. The 73% of those people who are forced to migrate are currently hosted in neighbouring countries. Turkey is located at the top of the list of countries who host the highest number of migrants, approximately reaching up to 3.6 million. Turkey is followed by Jordan (2.9 million), Colombia (1.8 million), Pakistan, Uganda and Lebanon (1.4 million), Germany (1.1. million), Sudan, Iran and Bangladesh (nearly 1 million). The 68% of migrants migrate from only 5 countries. These are: Syria (6.6 million), Venezuela (3.7 million), Afghanistan (2.7 million), South Sudan (2.2 million) and Myanmar (1.1 million).[4] When the GDP's of the aforementioned countries are compared, it is observed that Germany is the only country where the income per capita is over 10.000 USD and which is located at the north of 42nd parallel north.[5,6] Despite the fact that the number of migrants, the 40% of which is consisted of children, followed a horizontal course in the period of 1990-2015, the civil war in Syria and the economic and political instability erupted in Venezuela along with severe droughts caused by climate change and the scarcity of food has caused a sharp increase in the number of migrants and still remains at the peak point since 2015.

When looked at the group of countries or economic unions in which migrant movements are observed, it can be seen that nearly 26 million migrants tend to take shelter respectively in EU member states (2.5 million), OECD countries (7 million), low-income group of countries including Middle East or South Africa (9 million).[7]

---

[2] https://www.amnesty.org/en/what-we-do/refugees-asylum-seekers-and-migrants/global-refugee-crisis-statistics-and-facts/ (Access 24.11.2020).
[3] https://www.unhcr.org/figures-at-a-glance.html (Access 24.11.2020).
[4] ibid.
[5] https://www.amnesty.org/en/what-we-do/refugees-asylum-seekers-and-migrants/global-refugee-crisis-statistics -and-facts/ (Access 24.11.2020).
[6] https://data.worldbank.org/indicator/NY.GDP.PCAP.CD?most_recent_value_desc=true (Access 03.11.2020).
[7] https://data.worldbank.org/indicator/SM.POP.REFG?name_desc=true. (Access 05.11.2020).

Before delving into the policies of international trade organizations on migration and refugees, the conceptual framework of regional cooperation and international trade organizations will be discussed next.

Regional Cooperation and International Trade Organizations

In the post-World War II period, states preferred to act together in collaboration in order to liberalize the disrupted and reduced world trade, to repair their war-torn economies and to establish a new financial system. With this intention at hand, states took action by creating a number of cooperation and making special trade agreements and establishing trade blocks in order to achieve their common goal of sustaining international trade liberalization.

Aim of Regional Cooperation

Countries are more inclined towards participating in economic integrations with the purposes of resisting the highly complicated competition conditions as well as increasing their production capacities and performances.[8] The importance of economic integrations which aim to catalyse the economic relations between countries that are geographically in close proximity increase day by day on the account of these countries' efforts in resisting the increasing competition conditions and their desire of having a say in globalizing markets. When the common goals of regional economic cooperation are evaluated, the following main themes attract attention:[9]

- Through economic cooperation, particularly the production capacities, resource efficiencies and the levels of social welfare of developing countries are increased in a way to bring their insufficient national markets up to a level where they can manage to compete with industrialized countries;

- Through regional economic integration, foreign trade volume is increased, source distribution is activated hence contribute to the welfare development of member countries;

- Competitive power against exterritorial blocks is strengthened and clash of interests among countries within the same region are prevented;

- Regional instabilities are overcome, countries that are united in political matters are given a chance to raise their concerns, and

---

[8] Bahar Şanlı "Ekonomik Entegrasyon Teorisi Çerçevesinde Avrasya Birliği'nin Olabilirliği", **İktisadi ve İdari Bilimler Dergisi**, Cilt. 22, Sayı. 1, 2008.
[9] C. Erdem Hepaktan ve Serkan Çınar, "Küreselleşmenin Ekonomik Entegrasyon Üzerine Etkileri", International Conference on Eurasian Economies, 2011, p. 68.

mutual solutions to common social-political problems are found;

- Factors such as cross-border factor movements between countries, coordination of monetary and financial policies, full employment targets, high levels of economic growth and better income distribution are brought into the forms of integrated goals.

Types of Regional Economic Integrations

Regional economic integrations can be analysed under five different categories: free trade areas, customs unions, common markets, economic unions, and political unions.[10]

Free Trade Area: They are based on agreements among member states that allow for the free movement of goods in a specified trade area by eliminating trade barriers such as tariffs and quotas applied to the exchange of commodities.[11] The previous customs tariffs applied by the member states to countries that are excluded from the agreement continue to be applied in the same way. European Free Trade Association (EFTA), Latin American Free Trade Association (LAFTA) and European Economic Space (EES) are just a few examples of this type of economic integration. In free trade areas, the common market created for the incoming goods and services is not open to the production factors; and the harmonization of economic policies and institutions is not an option. The main of free trade area is the creation of a common market in which trade on goods and services are liberalized among the member states.

Custom Union: In addition to the elimination of all trade barriers among each other, the countries which form the union also apply a common customs tariff to third countries.[12] The first example to this type of integration can be identified as the customs union called Zollverein created by the German states back in 1834. The European Economic Community established in 1957 is another good example of a customs union.[13] In the stage of a customs union, neither the transnational mobility of production factors nor the unification of economic policies are attained. As a regional integration type, customs union which is based upon the principle of non-application of customs, represents an advanced level of integration in which the member states are forbidden to follow independent free trade policies in

---

[10] Canan Çetin, **Temel İşletmeciliğe Giriş**, 4. Baskı, İstanbul, Beta Yayınevi.
[11] Aydın Sarı, "Bölgelerarası Ekonomik Entegrasyonlar ve Türkiye'nin Ödemeler Bilançosuna Etkileri", **Süleyman Demirel Üniversitesi İktisadi ve İdari Bilimler Fakültesi Dergisi**, Cilt. 10, Sayı. 1, 2005, p. 119.
[12] İbid., p. 119.
[13] Şanlı, ibid., p. 16.

addition to their compliance for the conditions applicable to free trade area.[14]

Single/Common Market: The third stage in economic integration is the single/common market. As a natural outcome of customs union, if the production factors such as labour, capital and enterprising freely move among the union, and if the conditions for customs union are applied without any restrictions then a common market is supposedly established between the member states. The most successful example of a single/common market is considered as the European Union.[15] Four main freedoms are applicable within the scope of a single/common market. These are listed as:[16]

- Free movement of goods,
- Free movement of people,
- Free movement of capital,
- Free movement of services.

Economic Union: The final stage of economic integration is the economic union. The full integration of the economies of member states is expected at this stage. In addition to the conditions attained at the earlier stages of integration, the full unification of economic, monetary and social policies along with relevant institutions is expected in an economic union. It also involves a single monetary system and the establishement of a central bank along side of a fiscal system and common foreign trade policies.

Political Union: The harmonization of monetary and fiscal policies of countries requires for central administration in economic terms. The union that takes joint actions on economic issues will eventually pave the way for full integration encompassing various matters such as securty and defence. Political union involves implementations on common political and legal values, relative cultural homogenity, prospective target density, common structures that manage conditions of economic-monetary union, as well as mechanisms that trigger partnership.[17]

Whilst the free trade area represents the lowest level of cooperation, political union is considered as the deepest and most comprehensive level of regional integration.[18]

---

[14] Elmin İsayev, "Bölgesel Entegrasyonların Başarı Durumu Yönünden AB'nin Değerlendirilmesi", **Çankırı Karatekin Üniversitesi Uluslararası Avrasya Strateji Dergisi**, Cilt. 2, Sayı. 2, 2009.
[15] Şanlı, ibid., p. 16.
[16] İsayev, ibid., p. 199.
[17] İbid., p. 199.
[18] Hepaktan & Çınar, ibid., p. 68.

International Trade Organizations

The solid attempts to increase the volume of trade that shrank dramatically after World War II, and to recover the war-torn economies without a doubt impacted on the whole world. A number of inter-states cooperation and integration processes have been initiated with the aim of increasing trade volume, poverty reduction and increasing social welfare. Regional trade cooperation occupies an important place in the scope of these integration processes. The organizations established for the purpose of attaining member states the ability to act mutually and gain resistance towards competition in that respect has a supportive character. The organizations that are established for this purpose are geographically classified as listed below:[19]

Europe: European Free Trade Association (EFTA), European Union (EU), Black Sea Economic Cooperation Region (BSEC) and Commonwealth of Independent States.

Asia: Association of Southeast Asian Nations (ASEAN), Economic Cooperation Organization (ECO), Gulf Cooperation Council (GCC), MASHRIQ established by Egypt, Syria, Jordan and Lebanon for economic and political purposes, Asia-Pacific Economic Cooperation (APEC) and Organization of Islamic Cooperation (OIC).

America: Latin American Free Trade Association (LAFTA) (its name was changed in 1980 as Latin American Integration Association – LAIA/ALADI), Andean Pact established with the signing of Cartagena Agreement in 1969, Central American Common Market (CACM), the Caribbean Community (CARICON), North American Free Trade Agreement (NAFTA), the Southern Common Market (MERCOSUR) established by Brazil, Argentina, Paraguay and Uruguay in 1991.

Africa: Economic Community of West African States (ECOWAS), Central African Customs and Economic Union (UDEAC), Common Market for Eastern and Southern Africa (COMESA).

The approaches of international trade organizations that are broad in scope on the matter of immigration will be discussed next.

European Union (EU)

The EU is founded in 1951 by Belgium, the Netherlands, Luxemburg (BENELUX), Germany, France and Italy under the name of European Coal and Steel Community (ECSC) with the aim of developing coal and steel industries. In 1957, as a result of further integration in different sectors,

---

[19] Bahar Şanlı, "Küreselleşme ve Ekonomik Entegrasyonlar", **Doğu Anadolu Bölgesi Araştırmaları**, 2004, p. 165.

European Economic Community (EEC) was established; which later in 1992 transformed into a supranational organization called the European Union (EU) representing an exceptional example for economic and political integration as we know today. Except a few countries, most of the EU member states use a shared currency called "Euro". The EU which has been evolving since the very first day of its establishment, has reached to 28 member states with the inclusion of Croatia in 2013 whilst turning itself into a region of free movement with a population reaching up to 510 million European citizens. Brussels is considered as the de facto capital of the EU. The EU not only develop common policies related to economy, but also agriculture, industry, energy, political and security fields as well.[20]

The number of migrants reaching to the EU member states increased to 676.250 over the course of 10 years from 232.260 starting in 2009. The top 5 nationality of the migrants who apply for the EU are as follows: Syrian 12.1%), Afghans (8.6%), Venezuelans (7.3%), Colombians (5.2%) and Iraqis (4.4%). The top 5 EU member state that receive the highest number of applications are: Germany (142.400), France (119.900), Spain (115.200), Greece (74.900) and Italy (35.000).[21]

The Association of Southeast Asian Nations (ASEAN)

ASEAN was found in Bangkok by Indonesia, Malesia, the Philippines, Singapore and Thailand in 1967 after the founding members signed an agreement also known as the Bangkok Declaration. The founding purpose of ASEAN indicates that this organization prioritized political objectives over economic ones due to the fact that ASEAN, in the course of its establishment, was formed as an organization standing against communism in Southeast Asia.

Although ASEAN did not show a significant development until 1975, against the unification of Vietnam and the threat it posed on to member states, the organization regenerated its functionality with the aim of supporting the economic, social and cultural developments of the countries in the region with the Treaty of Amity and Cooperation in Southeast Asia signed in Bali in February 1976. With this Treaty, ASEAN member states aimed to establish large-scale industrial facilities through production of agricultural and industrial property goods; liberalize trade through the elimination of trade barriers; get into third markets as a union; provide cooperation on financial issues and create a preferential trade region.[22]

---

[20] https://www.dunyaatlasi.com/avrupa-birligi-ab-nedir/ (Access 04.11.2020).
[21] https://ec.europa.eu/eurostat/statistics-explained/index.php/Asylum_statistics#Citizenship_of_first-time_ appli cants:_largest_numbers_from_Syria.2C_Afghanistan_and_Venezuela (Access 25.11.2020).
[22] Hepaktan & Çınar, ibid., p. 70.

Over the course of time, ASEAN has become to several enlargement rounds with the inclusion of Negara Brunei Darussalam in 1984, Vietnam in 1995, Laos and Burma in 1997, and Cambodia in 1999.[23,24]

According to the UNHCR, in Asia Pacific region, there are 3.5 migrants, 1.9 million internally displaced people, and 1.4 million stateless persons. It is reported that migrants are mainly originating from Myanmar and Afghanistan where the refugee population constitutes the largest prolonged situation throughout the world.[25] For more than 30 years the 96% of the Afghan refugees live in Iran and Pakistan who generously opened their doors to them. On the other hand, nearly 500.000 people are escaping Myanmar to seek protection from conflict and violence.[26]

North America Free Trade Area (NAFTA)

After three failed attempts, the United States of America (USA) and Canada signed a free trade agreement which entered into force in 1989; later in 1994, the agreement took its final form with the inclusion of Mexico in the union.

One of the primary reasons for the establishment of NAFTA is that all three countries had become interdependent on each other due to their economic and trade relations. The fundamental principle of NAFTA is that it envisages a cooperation at the level of free trade agreement in the course of economic integration process.

NAFTA not only constitutes a trading block among the three member countries, but it also serves for the USA's individual interest in transforming the economy of Mexico since it is seen as the main country of origin for irregular migration to the USA. The USA sees NAFTA as means to prevent the irregular migration movements from Mexico by economically developing the country and freeing it from the hegemony of drug cartels and human traffickers; and by turning it into a country with export surplus.

European Free Trade Area (EFTA)

EFTA is an agreement designed by 8 European countries in 1960. From past to present, EFTA has lost its raison d'être since most of its founding members have become members of the EU. At the present time, members of the EFTA cooperate with the EU through a bilateral free trade agreement; and since 1994, members of the EU and EFTA have been provided with free movement and transfer of goods, services and capital through the agreement

---

[23] Mutlu Yılmaz & Ahmet Özken, **Dış Ticarete Giriş**, Ankara, Gazi Kitapevi, 2015.
[24] https://asean.org/asean/about-asean/ (Access 04.11.2020).
[25] https://www.unhcr.org/figures-at-a-glance.html (Access 24.11.2020).
[26] https://www.unhcr.org/asia-and-the-pacific.html (Access 25.11.2020).

on European Economic Area (EAA). EFTA members Iceland and Lichtenstein have not applied for the EU membership by preference; and Norway opted out from the EU membership as a result of the referendum held in 1994. Switzerland in a similar vein, preferred to stay out of the EU as well.[27]

According to the Eurostat statistics, among the members of EFTA, Switzerland is the most migrant receiving country. Switzerland is followed respectively by Norway and Lichtenstein. The incoming migrant profile shows that 1 out of 4 applications belong to underage people while 70% of applications are made by male applicants; and Nigeria and Somali have the highest number of applications for migration to EFTA members.

Organization for Economic Co-operation and Development (OECD)

OECD is an international organization aiming for creating better policies of a better life. The primary responsibilities of its 36 members with democratic structures and market economies integrated with the globalized world economy involve the resolution of social and administrative problems, providing financial stability, cooperation on trade, technology, innovation, entrepreneurship and development; and assisting the governments on the fight against poverty. The members of the OECD apart from Turkey which one of its founding members, include the USA, Germany, Australia, Austria, Belgium, Czech Republic, Denmark, Estonia, Finland, France, the Netherlands, the UK, Ireland, Spain, Israel, Sweden, Switzerland, Italy, Iceland, Japan, Canada, The Republic of Korea, Latvia, Lithuania, Luxemburg, Hungary, Mexico, Norway, Poland, Portugal, Slovakia, Slovenia, Chile, New Zealand and Greece.[28]

According to the World Bank report of 2019, OECD members host nearly 7 million migrants. Turkey remains at the top of this list as it hosts more than 3.5 million migrants on its own. Turkey is followed respectively by Germany (1.1. million), France (407.915), the USA (341.715), Sweden (253.787). Among the members of OECD, the number of migrants is 331 in Estonia, 634 in Colombia, 665 in Latvia, 741 in Slovenia, and 894 in Iceland.[29]

Asia-Pacific Economic Cooperation (APEC)

APEC was established in 1989 with the aim of promoting free trade and sustainable development in the shore economies of the Pacific. In addition

---

[27] Svend Hollensen, **Global Marketing: A Decision-Oriented Approach,** 4th Edition, Prentice Hall, 2007.

[28] https://www.oecd.org/ (Access 25.11.2020).

[29] https://data.worldbank.org/indicator/SM.POP.REFG (Access 25.11.2020).

to that, APEC supported the establishment of other economic organizations such as NAFTA and the EU. 21 member economies of APEC include the USA, Australia, Negara Brunei Darussalam, Canada, Chile, Hong Kong, China, Indonesia, Japan, Malaysia, Mexico, New Zealand, Papua New Guinea, Peru, the Philippines, Russa, Singapore, The Republic of Korea, Taipei, Thailand and Vietnam.[30],[31] APEC countries constitute the 38% of world population with nearly 3 million people living.[32]

According to the report of Statista,[33] among the members of APEC, China hosts 303.379 migrants whereas Malaysia hosts 129.107; Thailand 97.556, Australia 76.768, Indonesia 10287, South Korea 3196 and Japan 1463 migrants respectively.

Mercosur

Mercado Común del Sur (Spanish) or Mercado Comum do Sul (Portugese) is a trade partnership forum which provides free movement of goods, services and people among its members in South America; and a forum which has a customs union. MERCOSUR was established in 1991 by the signing of a free trade area agreement among Argentina, Brazil, Paraguay and Uruguay. With the inclusion of Venezuela, MERCOSUR currently has five members; and its associate members include Bolivia (full member candidate), Ecuador, Colombia, Peru, and Chile.[34]

In 2000, the members and associate members of the South American trade block, MERCOSUR signed a comprehensive declaration on the strengthening of refugee protection in the whole region. Instead of a narrow definition that recognizes refugees on an individual basis, this declaration adopts a broader definition on refugees by including people subject to human rights violations as well as violence victims. The declaration refers to the need of Latin America on the harmonization of regulations and procedures on asylum; and it is accepted as an important milestone in the formation of a generous and strong refugee protection regime in the southern cone of South America.[35]

---

[30] https://www.state.gov/asia-pacific-economic-cooperation-apec/) (Access 25.11.2020).
[31] https://www.investopedia.com/terms/a/asiapacific-economic-cooperation-apec.asp (Access 25.11.2020).
[32] https://www.worlddata.info/alliances/apec-asia-pacific-economic-cooperation.php (Access 24.11.2020).
[33] https://www.statista.com/statistics/733820/asia-pacific-refugee-population-by-country/ (Access 24.11.2020).
[34] Kıvanç Sağır, "Mercosur", **Uluslararası Politika Akademisi**, http://politikaakademisi.org /2013/02/02/mercosur/ (Access 24.11.2020).
[35] https://www.unhcr.org/news/briefing/2000/11/3ae6b82358/unhcr-welcomes-south-america mercosur-declara tion.html (Access 24.11.2020).

Common Market for Eastern and South Africa (COMESA)

COMESA is consisted of 19 African countries that agreed upon a regional integration through trade enhancement. The member countries of COMESA include the Republic of Burundi, the Republic of Djibouti, Comoros, the Republic of Democratic Congo, Eritrea, Ethiopia, Kenya, Libya, Madagascar, Malawi, Mauritius, Egypt, Rwanda, the Seychelles, Sudan, Uganda, Zambia, and Zimbabwe.[36] The main purpose of COMESA is to provide peace and security, and to increase welfare through economic integration in the region.

The current strategy of COMESA is known as "economic welfare through regional integration"; principally aiming to form a wide regional and trading block that can overcome certain barriers that are experienced by each individual state. The COMESA members which follow a liberalization process since 1984 targeting the elimination of tariff and non-tariff barriers in the region, also cancelled out gradually the customs tariffs in accordance with the customs discount statements adopted in 1992. These countries also eliminated quota limitations and non-tariff barriers in order to attract investors, increase the volume of foreign trade and increase welfare.[37]

According to the international migration report of 2017, the number of international migrants in Africa has shown an increase more than 67%. Since 2000, the number of international migrants in COMESA has increased 48% until 2017, the numbers reaching to 8.7 million from 5.8 million. The migrant movements in this region show a rapid change due to various socio-economic, political and religious factors emerging in respective countries in the region. By mid 2017, COMESA countries hosted nearly 4 million refugees, whereas Ethiopia and Kenya alone hosted more than 1 million migrants in the same year.

The Impact of International Trade Organizations on the Refugee Crisis

Considering per capita income, except some of the small city-states and island-countries are as in Switzerland USD 81.993, in Ireland USD 78.661, in Norway USD 75.419, in Iceland USD 66.944, in Singapore USD 65.233, in the United States USD 65.118, in Denmark USD 59,822, in Australia USD 54,907, in Netherlands USD 52,447, in Sweden USD 51.610 and in Austria USD 50,277. The common ground of all of these countries are their integration into a strong customs union and a common market. (Ireland, Denmark, Netherlands, Sweden, Austria-EU; United States – NAFTA;

---

[36] Barbaros Demirci, "Comesa (Doğu ve Güney Afrika Tercihli Ticaret Bölgesi) ve EAC – (Doğu Afrika Topluluğu) Plastik ve Plastik İşleme Makineleri Dış Ticareti", http://www.pagev.org.tr /admin/PICS/ dosyalar/COMESA_ve_EAC_ULKELERI.pdf (Access 24.11.2020).

[37] Barbaros Demirci, ibid.

Switzerland, Norway, Iceland – EFTA; Singapore & Australia – APEC). Besides, another common point of those 11 countries which have the most developed Gross Domestic Product (GDP) per capita are at the bottom lines among the World countries in regard to the hosting refugees. The refugee's population hosted in these countries are; in Switzerland 110,162, in Ireland 7,795, in Norway 53,882, in Iceland 894, in Singapore 5, in the United States 341,715, in Denmark 37,533, in Australia 76,768, in Netherlands 94,417, in Sweden 253,787 and in Austria 135,951. Nevertheless, it is observed that Japan which has high GDP per capita and successful trade agreements hosts 1463 refugee people, New Zealand 2724 refugee people and Korea Rep. 3196 refugee people.[38]

Among the World top refugee host countries, looking at the countries hosting the largest refugee population; Turkey has GDP per capita USD 9042, Jordan USD 4330, Pakistan USD 1284, Lebanon USD 7784 and Uganda USD 776 were being reported; even though those countries are not replaced as members in economic integration as much successful as in the first group, (Turkey – Custom Union with EU, OPEC, the Organization of Islamic Co-operation; Jordan & Lebanon – Arab League and the Organization of Islamic Co-operation; Pakistan – The Economic Cooperation Organization, the Organization of Islamic Co-operation; Uganda – COMESA, East African Community and the Organization of Islamic Co-operation)[39] they have cooperation with particular trade organizations in their geographical areas. It is observed that the common points of the displaced people who have been moved to cross their national boundaries are beside the ongoing civil-war and unrest, their GDP per capita are below USD 1500 and they are not being included in the strong economic integration.

Conclusion

It is observed that the original countries of the refugee people who have been forced to move or displace were generally not able to establish a strong economic integration with their neighbours or regional countries. Nevertheless, it is observed on the reports of official and non-governmental publications that the countries which are economically and commercially strong and have high GDP per capita are not hosting high refugee population, relatively the countries below USD 10,000 are hosting more refugee population. Only Venezuela can be regarded apart from this sampling. The country has above USD 15,000 GDP per capita in the year

---

[38] https://data.worldbank.org/indicator/SM.POP.REFG?most_recent_value_desc=false (Access 26.11. 2020).
[39] https://data.worldbank.org/indicator/NY.GDP.PCAP.CD?most_recent_value_desc=true (Access 26.11.2020).

2014 and has an important petroleum and natural gas reserve but because of the internal political instability and USD origin coup attempt, the country had a turndown and country's population had to migrate to neighbour countries foremost Colombia. On the other side, looking at the immigrant hosting countries, it is observed that Germany is the only exceptional country with high GDP per capita, especially is hosting high population Turkish immigrants.

In regard to the relations between International Commercial Organizations and immigrants; any regular or irregular migration movement has not been observed from countries which have successful economic integration; besides, the countries which have strong economy and high GDP are at the bottom lines for hosting refugee population.